Sledding in Avalanche Terrain: Reducing the Risk

Bruce Jamieson,

Darcy Svederus and

Lori Zacaruk

Published by

P.O. Box 2759, Revelstoke, BC V0E 2S0 Canada

Phone 1-250-837-2435, Fax 1-250-837-4624

info@avalanche.ca   www.avalanche.ca

ISBN 978-0-9781741-2-5

Printed in Canada

©2007 Canadian Avalanche Association

Revelstoke, British Columbia, Canada

Design and layout by Snowline Techinical Services and Brent Strand

Illustrations by Bruce Jamieson

Cover design by Bruce Jamieson

Front cover photo by Dusty Veideman, Photo House, Revelstoke, BC

Back cover photos by Lori Zacaruk (lower) and Darcy Svederus (upper)

Printed in Canada by Kromar Printing Ltd.

Library and Archives Canada Cataloguing in Publication

Jamieson, James Bruce

Sledding in avalanche terrain : reducing the risk / Bruce Jamieson, Darcy Svederus and Lori Zacaruk. -- 2nd ed.

Includes bibliographical references and index.

ISBN 978-0-9781741-2-5

1. Snowmobiling--Safety measures. 2. Avalanches--Safety measures. I. Svederus, Darcy, 1959- II. Zacaruk, Lori, 1968- III. Canadian Avalanche Association IV. Title.

QC929.A8J33 2007   796.94'0289   C2007-907576-2

Preface

This book is the second edition of *Sledding in Avalanche Terrain: Reducing the Risk*. Lori Zacaruk joins Darcy Svederus and Bruce Jamieson in this edition. She brings vast experience in teaching avalanche safety courses to sledders. The book includes many new photos and has been updated for compatibility with the Canadian Avalanche Centre's course outlines for Avalanche Skills Training Courses.

We have used superscripts like this[1] to mark facts and ideas from other sources. In some cases these references may help readers dig deeper into the subject, but we also want to recognize the contributions of others to avalanche education.

In time, this edition will be revised. We look forward to comments from readers and avalanche instructors.

Acknowledgements

Many people reviewed and commented on drafts or earlier versions of this book. For their help we are grateful to Doug Chabot, Helene Steiner, Cam Campbell, Randy Zacaruk, Pascal Haegeli as well as Dwayne Paynton and Dan Pecora of the BC Snowmobile Federation, Lyle Birnie, Wes Eror, Glen Gillis, Louise Sherren, Rosalie Svederus and Bill Warren of the Alberta Snowmobile Association, Phil Hein, Randy Stevens, Alan Dennis, Evan Manners, Jim Bay and Tim Quinn.

We are very grateful to Tracey Telford for writing a personal account of an avalanche that caught her and her partner.

This updated book is part of a project to reduce the number of people injured and killed by avalanches. The Canadian Avalanche Association is grateful to Yamaha Mortorsports for assisting with the publication of this book.

Bruce Jamieson, Darcy Svederus and Lori Zacaruk

Table of Contents

Chapter 1
Introduction

Snowmobiling in the mountains, like many enjoyable things in life, involves risk. If we are sledding on or below slopes steeper than 25°, there is a risk being caught by an avalanche. But just as there are things we can do to reduce the risk of vehicle crashes, there are things we can do to reduce the risk of getting caught, injured and perhaps killed by avalanches while sledding in the mountains.

Rescue training is an key component of avalanche courses. Lori Zacaruk photo.

These actions include

• taking an avalanche course

• getting information on current weather and avalanche conditions before we go

• having rescue equipment and practicing rescue skills

• observing the weather and avalanche conditions

• choosing routes and slopes appropriate to the conditions

• choosing good riding partners and practices for low-risk sledding.

Some riders will assess the conditions and select low-risk routes for the current conditions. They will probably be enjoying the mountains for many years without getting caught in any avalanches large enough to hurt them. Others will choose higher risk routes and slopes for the current conditions.

They are more likely to trigger and get caught in an avalanche. With or without knowing it, they are gambling that the motion of the avalanche won't fatally injure them, and that their fellow riders have the skills and equipment to find them before they suffocate. The danger is real: From 1999 to 2007, an average of about 13 sledders were killed annually by avalanches in North America[1]. About twenty-five percent of avalanche victims are fatally injured by the motion of the avalanche or by hitting rocks, trees or the ground[2,3,4]. Roughly another 25% suffocate within half an hour.

In this book we will explain the odds of surviving an avalanche, what to do if caught, and what others should do if you are caught. More importantly, we hope this book helps you develop the riding habits and decision-making for many years of enjoyable mountain riding—within your level of risk.

This book is not a substitute for an avalanche course. We encourage readers to take an avalanche course that includes field training, a safe snowmobiling/survival course, and first aid training.

While we strongly recommend avalanche training, keep in mind that avalanche books and courses cover only the basics of assessing avalanche danger and reducing avalanche risk. Afterwards, much remains to be learned from experienced sledders, the snowpack and the mountains.

These riders are avoiding avalanche terrain. It's a good option when the avalanche danger is considerable or higher. Maybe not as challenging as the steep slopes... but better than being caught! Lori Zacaruk photo.

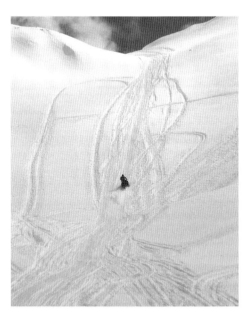

When hill climbing, riding one at a time means other riders won't get caught and can start the search if you are caught. Tim Klone photo.

Chapter 2
Avalanche! A First Person Account

by Tracey Telford

Butch Garrett died while snowmobiling, January 5th 1994 because I didn't have a transceiver, probe and shovel. Neither did he. He died because we didn't take nine hours of our busy schedule to take an avalanche awareness course. While high pointing ahead of me, he triggered a size 2.5 slide that buried him, his machine and mine completely, and me partially.

We were on our way down the mountain. It was dark and we had checked all the traps on the trap line. Butch was busy putting high marks on the bank beside the road. He would mark a few and stop and wait for me to follow along in his tracks. On the last one he turned and yelled for me to follow his mark up the slope. As I looked up it seemed as though the snow was coming down the bank towards me. I looked back at Butch and as he looked up the hill I watched the expression on his face change from one of carefree fun to one of disbelief and horror, that I have carried with me ever since.

He was engulfed in a wave of snow before I could raise my arm in a motion to signal "get going." My arm was up in the air when my own machine was hit and I felt it being lifted and carried over the edge of the

This photo shows a different cutblock than the one mentioned in the account. When a cutblock is steep enough and the stumps and slash have been smoothed over by snow (as in this photo), it deserves the same respect and assessment as any avalanche path. This includes plan your route to avoid terrain traps, cross one at a time, and watch from a safe place. Bruce Jamieson photo.

road. I fought to stand on my machine and keep above the snow that had just covered my legs and my waist. I stood and looked at the snow that had already gone around me; it was moving very fast towards the bottom of the dry lakebed. The snow was about to pull me off the machine and it was as if a voice from somewhere said, "You can stay with the machine or swim." I sat back down and hung on.

The avalanche stopped moving and an eerie silence settled in the darkness around me. I waited for Butch to call my name, while at the same time I knew that I would never hear his voice again. Shoving that unwanted knowledge as far back as I could, I dug myself out and crawled over the snow to search for him. I had only my hands to dig with and I spaced the holes as best I could. I dug many holes—one of them was six feet deep where I had last seen him. It was so deep that at one point I stopped and looked up and realized that if another avalanche let go, I had just dug my own grave. No one would ever find us.

I remember being really hot and wanting to peel off the layers of clothes that I had on—and did. I kept them all with me as I crawled along because I knew that I had a long walk out ahead of me. Even today I am amazed at how calm and rational I remained during search—if only I had

This photo is from a different fatal accident than the one in the account, but shows the damage avalanches can do. Overall about 20-25% of avalanche victims are killed by hitting trees, rocks or the ground or due to the turbulent avalanche motion itself. However, on short slopes without trees, more than 80% of people caught probably survive the avalanche forces. Their survival then depends mostly on the air space near their face and an efficient rescue by their companions. Jonty Caroe photo.

known the proper search and rescue techniques. The avalanche seemed to drop off really steep near the edge of the road and I was afraid to crawl over the edge and search the bottom half. I searched for what seemed to be hours, found many things like sticks, branches and logs. I never found Butch. He was found the next day with his machine on top of him—by a search and rescue dog, named Echo— near the bottom of the avalanche, only two feet under, with one hand inches from the surface.

I thought maybe I could ride out. So I crawled back across the boulders of the avalanche to my machine and dug down to the seat and the axe underneath it. I was hoping it would help me get through the snow as it was packed in around the machine like cement. It was even stuffed in the vents on the hood. Already exhausted, I was unable to uncover my snowmobile completely. I turned it on, but it didn't sound the same and I was afraid that the sound would trigger the rest of the snow above me so I shut it off. I sat there for a moment, wishing many things, wondering how far up the mountain we actually were and thankful that we were half-way down already. Most of all I wished that the small shovel, matches and flashlight were in my snowmobile instead of his.

I worked my way over to the edge of the avalanche. It was there that I sat and cried out my "I love you's" and "goodbyes." My own voice reaching out in the quiet little valley, a strange sad sound.

After 8 km of crying, stumbling, praying and hearing the branches in the bushes crack as if there was an animal following me, I finally reached the bottom of the mountain and the truck. I thought to myself that at least we chose to hide the keys on the truck and not put them in his coat pocket where he usually placed them.

Though I will never ride again I have taken the time to learn some of the things that I should have known before. I have spent many nights wondering why I never picked up and probed with the stick that I dug out while searching for him.

One time we were ice fishing up at Wolf Lake and we heard what sounded like a loud jet going overhead. We looked up into the back bowl and saw a huge avalanche come down the chute —what an amazing and frightening sight. Even after seeing one it never occurred to me that this could happen to us. It is the worst feeling in the world when someone's life depends on your very next move—and you fail.

***

Note: The technical details of this incident are reported on pages 124-125 of *Avalanche Accidents in Canada, Volume 4: 1984-96.*

These riders are practising avalanche rescue when they could be sledding. Safety equipment and rescue practice can make the difference. Lori Zacaruk photo.

Chapter 3
Formation and Nature of Avalanches

Avalanches range in size from small *sluffs* that would not harm a person to large slides capable of destroying villages and forests. In western Canada, it is estimated that over a million destructive avalanches occur per winter—most occur away from people and property. Sometimes mud, rock or timber are carried within an avalanche.

Types of avalanches

Avalanches release from snow slopes in two distinct ways. A **point release** or **loose snow avalanche** starts when a small amount of cohesionless snow—typically the size of a snowball—slips and begins to slide down a slope setting additional snow in motion.

Alternatively, a **slab avalanche** requires that a plate-like slab of cohesive (strong or well bonded) snow overlies a weak snow layer. The slab, which may consist of one or more layers, is released by fractures in the weak layer. The slab begins to slide as a unit before breaking up. Following a slab avalanche, a distinct fracture line or crown fracture is visible at the top of the slide. Slab avalanches are often a major hazard to sledders and other recreationists, The photos on the front and back covers are slab avalanches.

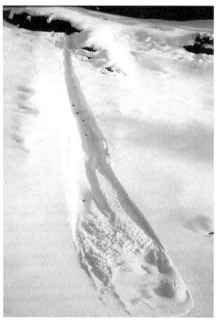

A small loose snow avalanche. These can be quite dangerous when they are large, wet or run into a terrain trap such as a creek bed. Bruce Jamieson photo.

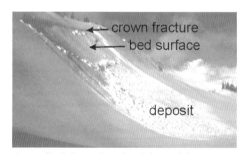

crown fracture
bed surface
deposit

A small slab avalanche. Most of the danger to sledders is due to slab avalanches. James Blench photo.

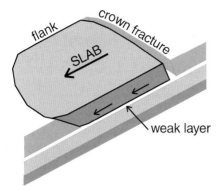

Slab avalanches require a cohesive slab consisting of one or more layers and a weak layer, although the weak layer is sometimes hard to find.

There are few hard-and-fast rules when dealing with avalanche characteristics. However, the following generalizations are useful:

- Slab avalanches are usually larger, more destructive and more difficult to predict than loose snow avalanches.

- Slab avalanches are sometimes triggered from the middle of the slope—making escape difficult.

- Slab avalanches are sometimes *remotely* triggered, i.e. by people who are **not** in the start zone of the avalanche.

- Avalanches involving harder, thicker slabs are generally less predictable and larger[3] than avalanches involving thinner, softer slabs.

- Most of the danger to sledders is due to **slab avalanches**.

Triggers

Most avalanches are triggered when slopes are loaded by additional snow. However, **about 90% of the avalanches that injure or bury people are triggered by people**[3], often by the victim or by a member of the same group. Often people start the fracture in the weak layer under the slab; the fracture spreads and releases the avalanche.

Natural triggers

- loading of slope by snowfall

- loading of slope by wind-deposited snow

- warming temperatures or rain

- cornice fall

- rockfall, etc.

Human and artificial triggers

- people moving on or near the slope

- snowmobiles,

- explosions, e.g. to re-open the highway, etc.

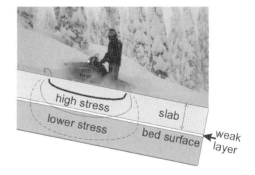

People and sleds cause stress in the underlying snowpack. This stress decreases with depth. Enough stress will sometimes start fractures in buried weak layers. These fractures often spread (propagate) far enough to release slab avalanches. Amber Wood photo.

Avalanche motion and forces

- Avalanche speeds range widely. Typically, dry slides can attain speeds of 50 to 200 km/h (30 to 120 mph) and wet slides, although usually slower, can attain speeds of 20 to 100 km/h[5] (12 to 60 mph).

- Most avalanches have a flowing component which consists of relatively dense snow flowing down the slope.

- When dry flowing avalanches exceed about 35 km/h (22 mph), a dust or powder cloud of airborne particles of snow moves above the flowing component[6].

- Forces are generally greatest in the flowing component of an avalanche near the ground[5].

- Most wet snow avalanches have little or no airborne component.

- Small wet avalanches can be surprisingly powerful and harmful.

A mixed motion avalanche. Once the powder cloud develops, it often hides the dense flow in the bottom metre (3 feet) or so of the avalanche. Small, slower avalanches or wet avalanches may not form a powder cloud. If caught, riders and sleds are carried by the dense flow, where the forces are greatest. When the avalanche stops, the deposit may be much deeper than a metre. Will Geary photo.

Mountain sleds—even when pointing away from the avalanche path—cannot out-run the larger and faster avalanches.

Chapter 4
Avalanche Terrain

Recognizing avalanche terrain

To avoid high avalanche risk, we often have to select routes and slopes that are appropriate for the current conditions. This requires that we recognize avalanche terrain and the factors that affect the avalanche danger on particular slopes.

The classic avalanche path consists of a start zone at the top of the path, followed by a narrower track down the slope with a less steep runout zone at the bottom of the path. The start zone is often steeper than the track and may be shaped or oriented so that it tends to accumulate wind-deposited snow.

Confined avalanche paths are easily recognized as an opening down through trees or between the walls of a gully. Other avalanche slopes, such as the ones on the the next page or the front and back covers of this book, are not so easily recognized.

When on or below slopes steep enough to produce avalanches, look for evidence of avalanches such as:

* fracture lines or avalanche deposits, or

* missing trees, broken-off trees, or trees with missing or broken branches.

Under certain snowpack conditions, avalanches can start on or run down many open slopes, bowls, chutes and sparsely treed slopes.

These trees have been damaged by avalanches. Usually there are better places to regroup. Bruce Jamieson photos.

Most of the challenging sledding and hill climbing is in avalanche terrain.

Many avalanche slopes do not have an obvious start zone, track and runout. Most of the shaded areas and some of the tracked slopes are steep enough for avalanches to start, but there are no trees or bushes to tell us how far avalanches have run from the start zones. Lori Zacaruk photo.

Slope angle of the start zone

Most avalanches that begin on slopes steeper than 60° are small, loose snow sluffs. Although they are usually small, these avalanches sometimes trigger larger slides on the slopes below.

Larger avalanches usually start on slopes between 30° and 60°. Most large slab avalanches begin on slopes between 30° and 45°. Less than 5% of slab avalanches[7] begin on slopes of less than 25°. Avalanches that *begin* on slopes of less than 25° usually consist of wet snow[8].

Perhaps the simplest way to avoid avalanches is by not traveling *on or below* slopes steeper than 30° when the snow is dry. However, this excludes too many fine routes and slopes for most riders. Many sledders want to run steep gullies to the next drainage or climb slopes over 30°, or even 40°. Reducing the risk on such terrain requires a careful consideration of the avalanche danger (Chapter 6) and safety measures (Chapter 7).

Usually, to measure the angle of the steepest part of a slope, we must expose ourselves to the slope, often from below! However, when the local avalanche danger is low, we can practice with a clinometer to help us improve our "eye" for slope angle.

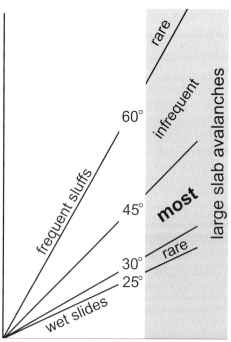

Most large slab avalanches start on 30 to 45° slopes—the same angles which are great for challenging mountain riding and hill climbing.

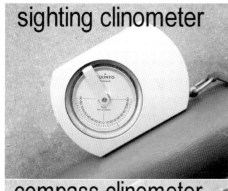

Wind blows up the windward slope removing snow and down the lee slope depositing the snow. The smooth wind-deposited snow on the lee slopes can remain unstable for days. Bruce Jamieson photo.

Orientation of slope to wind

Moderate and strong winds will distribute falling snow and redistribute loose snow from previous storms unevenly. Windward slopes (facing the wind) will receive less snow and may be left with a *scoured* appearance. Additional snow will be deposited on lee slopes (facing down-wind). This wind deposit may be pillow-shaped or chalky in appearance. Drifts called cornices sometimes form at the top of leeward slopes.

Inclinometers, clinometers or clinos. From the top or bottom of a slope you can look through the sighting clino (upper photo) and read the slope angle in degrees. When placed on the slope, the compass clino in the lower photo has a extra needle that hangs down, showing the slope angle in degrees. Both these uses require that you be on or close to the slope. Hence, both are best used to develop your "eye" for slope angle on days when avalanches are unlikely. Bruce Jamieson photos.

These wind deposits on lee slopes are very important for two reasons:

- snow will be deposited at several times the overall snowfall rate, which increases the load on weak layers and the likelihood of avalanches, and

- the wind-packed layers have the potential to release as slab avalanches, sometimes large ones.

These riders are using a compass clinometer to measure the slope angle. Lori Zacaruk photo.

Wind has blown snow from the right to the left in this photo. Some snow has been deposited in the cornice and more will be wind-loaded onto the slope below the cornice. The left part of this cornice is obviously unstable, but it is very difficult to tell how far to the right is supported by the ridge. If in doubt, stay well back from cornices. Bruce Jamieson photo.

The wind often deposits unstable snow slabs on lee slopes. Failing to recognize or under-estimating wind loading of lee slopes has contributed to many fatal

Wind blowing from left to right has loaded the slopes above these highmarks. The smooth "pillows" are the wind deposited snow. Phil Hein photo.

Orientation to sun

Sunny slopes

On sunny days, or when the sun radiates heat through thin clouds, snow on south-facing or sunny slopes will warm faster than snow on shady slopes. Sometimes, the snow surface on these sunny slopes will get sticky or wet—and avalanches will become more likely.

Snow conditions and avalanche danger are often quite different on the sunny slopes (right side of this photo) and shady slopes (left side). Lori Zacaruk photo.

Shady slopes

After storms, the new snow layers tend to remain unstable longer on shady and north-facing slopes than on sunny and south-facing slopes. This is because the snow on these shady slopes settles (and stabilizes) more slowly and because cool shady conditions favor the development of weak layers within the snowpack. Consequently, shady slopes are more likely to produce avalanches in cold, winter-like conditions.

Elevation

Typically, the avalanche danger is higher at higher elevations because there is more snowfall and more wind than at lower elevations. Also, at higher elevations there is less forest, which tends to anchor the snowpack. We often approach avalanche terrain from below and so we need to be continually alert for changing snow conditions and stability as we ascend.

Groomed trails and popular routes often pass through tracks and run out zones of large alpine paths.

Size of slope

Although there have been serious accidents on small slopes, larger slopes are usually more dangerous because they can produce larger avalanches. Regardless of the slope size, avalanche danger should always be assessed (Chapter 6) or the slope avoided. Should you decide to cross any avalanche slope, crossing quickly, one at a time, will help to reduce the risk.

Shape of slope

If you are uncomfortable with the avalanche danger on a particular slope, avoid it. However, if circumstances require that you cross such a slope, the shape of the slope can help you select your route across it.

The snow conditions at the top of the gully can be very different from conditions in the valley bottom—another reason to climb one at a time. Ray Mason photo.

In particular, the convex part of an slope (rolls, roll-overs or break-overs) should be avoided when you suspect unstable snow because these slopes are most easily triggered by sledders at, or slightly below, the convex part of the slope. Generally, it is best to cross the top of slope above the convex region.

Noting the hazard from above, these riders have stopped well back from the base of the slope. Note the small wet slides from the rock outcrops. Lori Zacaruk photo.

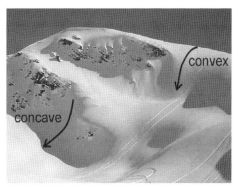

Complex terrain like this typically includes convex and convex areas, and often terrain traps. Claude LeGroulx photo.

Similarly, the safest place to cross a concave slope is often at the top. A sled is more likely to trigger an avalanche from high on a concave slope than from a lower position. However, should a slide occur, a rider caught low on the slope is more likely to be injured or buried than someone caught near the top.

Keep in mind that a slope may contain more than one convex or concave area, or a combination of the two shapes.

Gullies and bowls

Bowls and sometimes gullies may offer fine sledding when the avalanche danger is low. However, they are generally more dangerous than neighboring slopes for several reasons:

- In gullies and small bowls, there is usually no route to escape from an approaching avalanche.

- Riders caught in a gully by an avalanche will get pushed into the centre of the gully where the forces are highest and a deep burial is likely.

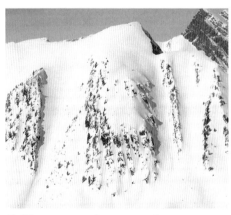

*Gullies are very dangerous places to get caught. It is a good idea to avoid gullies unless you are **sure** the snow is stable. ASARC photo.*

- A gully or the sides of a bowl may be loaded with snow by wind from any one of **several different directions.**

- Even if one side of a bowl has stable snow or has avalanched, travel in the bowl may not be safe because the snow on other sides of the bowl may be unstable.

- The fairly rapid effect of sun-warming, or the long-term effect of shade may reduce the snow stability on a particular side of a gully or bowl.

Terrain roughness

Bushes and rocks that stick through the snow or cause bumps in the snowpack tend to anchor layers of *cohesive* snow[8]. However, such a rough ground cover *does not guarantee* that the snow slope will not avalanche.

Slab avalanches can occur where the snowpack is thin if the ground is smooth (no anchors), as in this photo. The snowpack is often weaker, especially in mid-winter, where the snowpack is shallow, e.g. less than 1 metre (3 feet.). Bruce Jamieson photo.

The stabilizing effect of a rough ground cover is lost when additional snow has smoothed over the bumps from rocks and bushes. Also, *loose snow avalanches* may occur when the bumps, rocks and bushes are still visible.

These riders have stopped below mature trees to watch a fellow rider hill climbing. The undamaged branches on the trees indicate that avalanches rarely reach this parking place. Lori Zacaruk photo.

Avalanches don't often start in mature forests, but if they start above the forest, they can run through it, often removing the lower branches from trees. The avalanche in this photo ran through the forest and also down the adjacent open slope. People can be seriously injured or killed if they are carried into trees by avalanches. Bruce Jamieson photo.

Timber

Although mature timber is usually a good indicator of safe areas, riders should be looking for damage to vegetation and other evidence of avalanches. In winters with heavy snowfall, deep weak layers or strong winds, large avalanches may run farther than usual, smashing into forests and creating new paths or extending existing runout zones.

Islands of safety

Small groups of trees or large rocks that provide limited shelter from avalanches are often called "islands of safety". When crossing a wide slide path, stopping at such islands may be the only practical way one rider can watch others cross more exposed parts of the path.

Terrain traps

About 25% of avalanche fatalities are caused by physical injuries[2,3,4]. A terrain trap is any terrain feature that makes injuries or burial more likely, or makes escape from an approaching avalanche more difficult. In other words, a small avalanche combined with a terrain trap can have the same effect as a large avalanche.

Terrain traps include:

- gullies (including "chokes" where avalanche paths narrow), cliffs and crevasses since they make escape more difficult and because they concentrate the forces on the victim,

- flats or lakes at the bottom of steep slopes that may accumulate a deep avalanche deposit on top of an avalanche victim,

- snowmobile trails cut into side hills,

- creeks beds,

- cliffs or rock bands, and

- trees and large rocks in slide paths since they are likely to cause physical injuries to persons caught in the avalanche.

Gullies concentrate avalanche forces, make escape difficult and often leads to deep burials. The sequence of photos inside the front cover shows a rider who was unable to escape in the narrow part of the gully but was able to get to the side of the gully when the avalanche slowed and spread out.

Creek beds are one type of terrain trap because an avalanche can deeply bury a person. Even without an avalache, open creeks can be a serious hazard. Lori Zacaruk photo.

This avalanche deposited deep snow on the abrupt transition to the flats at the bottom of the slope. The rider dug from the hole did not survive. Darcy Svederus photo.

Slab avalanches are often more easily triggered from areas where the slab is thin.Wind blowing from right to left, has thinned the slab at the sides of the avalanche. The slab was a metre (3 feet) thick in the middle. In this photo, the slab is the entire snowpack and released on a layer of large weak crystals (depth hoar) at the base of the snowpack. Bruce Jamieson photo.

Sledder and riders discussing terrain and routes. Bruce Jamieson photo.

Snow conditions will vary from the lower slopes below treeline to the upper slopes near the ridge. Often the avalanche danger is higher above treeline than below. When riding below avalanche paths the hazard from above must be considered. Lori Zacaruk photo.

Summary

The three main terrain factors that affect avalanche danger are: slope angle, orientation to wind, and terrain traps.

Most dry slab avalanches start on slopes over 30°, usually over 35°.

The wind often deposits unstable wind slabs on the down-wind (lee) side of ridges, so windward slopes are often safer than leeward slopes. Failing to recognize or under-estimating wind loading of lee slopes has contributed to many avalanche accidents[9].

Getting caught in a terrain trap such as a gully, or getting carried into one, reduces your chance of survival.

Avalanches may be triggered from the particularly weak snow often found next to rocks, trees or bushes. Clearly, such features are not islands of safety[10].

The route following the solid line avoids starting zones and is therefore lower risk than the route follow the dashed line. Bruce Jamieson photo.

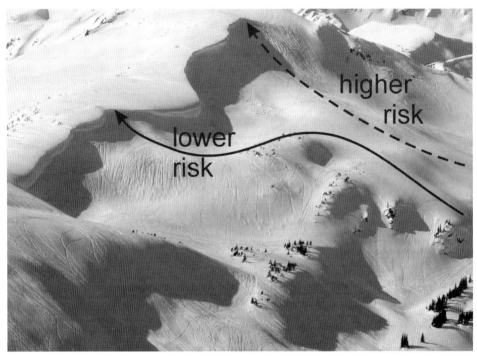

As with the photo above, the climb following the solid line is lower risk than the dashed line climb. Of course, the climb up the dashed line is probably a better test of a rider's skill and sled, but best left for a day when then the local avalanche danger is low. Lori Zacaruk photo.

Canadian Supplement to Chapter 4

Avalanche Terrain Ratings

To help backcountry users assess the seriousness of a route or area, especially when planning a trip to a new area, Parks Canada developed the Avalanche Terrain Exposure Scale in 2004. The ratings can give riders a first impression of the seriousness of a route.

Avalanche terrain is rated as either **Simple, Challenging** or **Complex.**

The Canadian Avalanche Centre and Park Canada have classified many of the most popular backcountry trips according to the Avalanche Terrain Exposure Scale. Go to *avalanche. ca* to see ratings for some popular snowmobile trips.

Simple terrain

Exposure to low angle or primarily forested terrain. Some forest openings may involve the runout zones of infrequent avalanches. Many options to reduce or eliminate exposure. No glacier travel. Lori Zacaruk photo.

Challenging terrain

Exposure to well defined avalanche paths, starting zones or terrain traps; options exist to reduce or eliminate exposure with careful routefinding. Glacier travel is straightforward but crevasse hazard may exist. Bruce Jamieson photo.

Complex terrain

Exposure to multiple overlapping avalanche paths or large expanses of steep, open terrain; multiple avalanche starting zones or terrain traps below; minimal options to reduce exposure. Complicated glacier travel with extensive crevasse bands or icefalls. Lori Zacaruk photo.

Chapter 5
Mountain Snowpack

A slab avalanche requires a weak layer underneath one or more layers of stronger or more cohesive snow. This chapter begins by considering the formation of strong and weak layers within the snowpack, so that we know where to look for slab conditions, i.e. for strong snow on top of a weak layer. The latter part of this chapter outlines how recent weather can increase or decrease the snow stability.

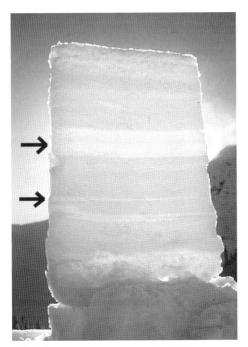

Weak layers are necessary for slab avalanches. This photo shows both thick and thin weak layers. Jim Bay photo.

The strength of storm snow layers

Layers of newly fallen snow vary in strength. Strong layers of new snow often consist of:

- wind-packed snow,

- dense snow, or

- snow which was deposited near 0°C (32°F).

Weak layers of new snow often consist of unbroken star-shaped crystals—especially large ones—or crystals shaped like needles or plates.

The strength of old snow layers

After new snow crystals have been on the ground for as little as a few hours to a few days, they change, or metamorphose into grains of old snow. Corresponding to these changes in grain shape and size, layers of snow either increase or decrease in strength.

Being able to find strong and weak snow layers in the field is helpful for assessing snow stability. Understanding how strong and weak layers are formed is much less important and is summarized in Appendix B.

The more important factors that change the strength of snow layers are:

Load

The more snow on top of a layer, the more the layer tends to strengthen. For *peristent* weak layers of relatively large angular crystals, this is a slow process that can take weeks.

Snowpack thickness and air temperature

Air temperatures close to but below freezing combined with a thick snowpack favor strengthening of snowpack layers (Appendix B). Hence, weak layers often stabilize faster in the spring.

On the other hand, a thin snowpack and cold temperatures often promote weakening of snowpack layers by faceting (Appendix B). Where the snowpack is thin, say less than a metre (3'), a week of cold temperatures may weaken snow layers noticeably. The resulting layers of *faceted crystals or depth hoar* (Appendix B) may remain weak for a month or more.

Subsequent snowfalls may add sufficient load causing slab avalanches to slide on weak layers of faceted crystals or depth hoar.

> *Thick weak layers are easier to find in the snowpack than thin weak layers, but thick or thin weak layers can release avalanches. The snowpack tests described in Chapter 6 can help us find thin weak layers.*

Warming, melting and freezing

When snow layers warm to near 0°C (32°F), they weaken.

At 0°C (32°F), snow may be moist or wet, and the wetter it is, the weaker it is.

When wet snow freezes, it becomes a relatively strong crust.

When the wet surface layer(s) freeze into a crust, avalanches will become less likely. If the crust warms and becomes wet, avalanches will become more likely. Lori Zacaruk photo.

Surface hoar

If the sky is relatively clear and the wind is light, it only takes one or two cool nights to form a beautiful layer of sparkling frost called surface hoar (or hoarfrost) on top of the snowpack. When the surface hoar is buried by subsequent snowfalls, it will form a weak layer that can reduce snow stability for weeks, and sometimes a month or more. Buried surface hoar layers are thin and often hard to find in the snowpack.

> *Surface hoar, faceted crystals and depth hoar are considered **persistent** weak layers.*

Large surface hoar crystals on tree and snow surface. Once buried, surface hoar layers often remain unstable for several weeks. Bruce Jamieson photo.

Regional differences in snowpack

In the mountains of Canada and the United States west of the Rockies, the snowpack is generally thicker and the air somewhat milder than in the Rockies. This effect of snowpack thickness and temperature can be understood by comparing the layering common to thick and thin snowpacks.

> *In the Interior Ranges of BC, many fatal avalanches have started in weak layers of buried surface hoar[12].*

West of the Rockies, the thickness of the snowpack and the generally warmer temperatures will cause most layers to become dense and strong over time.

During early and mid-winter in the Rockies when the snowpack is usually thin and the air cold, weak layers of faceted grains often form near the surface of the snowpack. Also, a weak layer of relatively large crystals called

Local differences in Snowpack

Anywhere the snowpack is thin—near a ridgetop or over a rock outcrop or bush—the snowpack may be weakened by faceting. Consequently, while walking or sledding, we sometimes break deeply into weak snow near a buried rock or bush.

Although we can never anticipate every hidden weak spot in the snowpack, we should "think terrain" and try to avoid weak spots. Not only is it tiring to get the sled out of weak

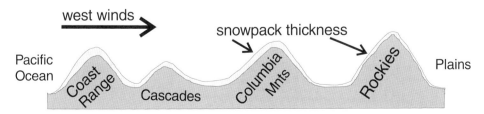

Snowfall decreases from west to east as moist air masses from the Pacific Ocean lose their moisture. Also, the snowpack is typically thicker on the western sides of these ranges than on their eastern sides.

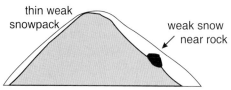

Weak snow is likely where the snowpack is thin near the ridge and over the rock.

snow, the fractures that release slab avalanches are sometimes triggered in these hidden weak spots.

Effect of recent weather on snow stability

Weather factors that decrease snow stability

- snowing hard—more than 2 cm (1") per hour—for a few hours

- rain

- moderate or strong winds (noticeable drifting)

- warming of the snow surface to 0°C (32°F) by solar radiation, warm wind or rain

- 30 cm (12") or more of snow within the last two days.

Weather factors that tend to increase snow stability

- cooling trend, especially after a thaw

- several days of moderate temperatures that allow the snow from the most recent storm to settle and strengthen.

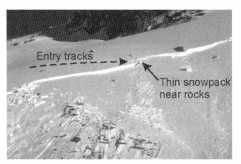

Slab avalanches, like this one, are sometimes triggered from thin areas, Also, weak faceted snow can develop near rocks that stick up into the snowpack. Phil Hein photo.

Wind blowing from the left is rapid loading —and increasing the avalanche danger— on the lee slopes. Bruce Jamieson photo.

Chapter 6
Recognizing Avalanche Risk

Avalanche Risk

Avalanche risk depends on terrain, snow stability and people. Since much of the good sledding is in avalanche terrain, the risk often depends on snow stability, we need to closely monitor the snow stability. This attention to snow stability starts with the regional bulletins.

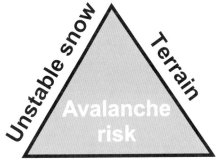

Without all three components: unstable snow, avalanche terrain and people, there is no avalanche risk. So, when the snow is unstable we can reduce our risk by avoiding avalanche terrain.

Snowmobiles can be an asset or a liability. Due to the large amount of terrain that a typical snowmobiler covers in a day, when there are areas of unstable snow—there often are—the odds are high that an *unaware* sledder may trigger an avalanche.

However, we need to use the sled to our advantage—to reduce the risk. We don't have to climb every hill every day. With such great access to terrain, riders can pick and choose their slopes. Although we can never be sure about snow stability, we can consistently choose slopes that the bulletin and our local observations indicate are likely stable and avoid those with higher hazard or terrain traps. In this way, a rider can still have a technically challenging day while avoiding the obvious high risk areas.

Making decisions based on regional information and local observations

This chapter reviews the regional bulletin and weather used for planning a trip and then focuses on local weather, snowpack and avalanche observations.These local observations all reflect *variations in weather and especially snowpack over the terrain.*

Often technically challenging terrain and good play areas can still be found on days when the avalanche danger is a concern. Tim Klone photo.

The chapter outlines some human factors than can compromise decisions, and gives three examples of reducing avalanche risk by selecting terrain according to the regional bulletin and local observations.

Snowpack and previous weather

The snowpack is a record of the winter's weather. For example, major snowstorms result in thick layers; thaws and rainstorms result in moist layers or crusts; and periods of cold, clear weather sometimes result in a layer of surface hoar (frost) or a snow layer weakened by faceting (Appendix B).

Before starting a trip, ask locals and the staff at information centres about previous weather and the snowpack (and terrain). For example, reports of a buried layer of surface hoar or slab avalanches occurring many days after a storm, indicate that a persistent weak layer exists in the snowpack. These layers can remain unstable and unpredictable for weeks after they are buried by snowfall.

Avalanche bulletins

Avalanche bulletins are available for many mountain areas. For current lists of regional bulletins, see www. avalanche.ca (Canada) or www. avalanche.org (USA).

Sources include recorded telephone messages and various web sites. Sometimes this information is available in newspapers or on the

Fresh avalanches, no matter what size, are the surest sign of unstable snow. Shelly Markiwsky photo.

radio or TV. Before traveling in or near an area for which public avalanche information is available, the information should be obtained and discussed among the group.

Most avalanche information agencies rate the avalanche danger using five levels: *low, moderate, considerable, high* or *extreme* (Appendix C).

Riders with limited experience assessing snow stability should err on the side of caution when selecting terrain.

Field observations

While on the way to the staging area and while sledding, observe the following clues to the snowpack stability:

Avalanches

Note the direction the slope faces (the aspect) and elevation of any fracture lines or avalanche deposits and estimate how long ago they occurred. Recent avalanches mean the snowpack is currently unstable.

Effects of wind

- Drifts, cornices or smooth pillows of snow indicate where snow has been deposited. More snow means we should expect more avalanches.

- Wind scouring (or sastrugi), usually on the windward slopes and ridge tops indicates where the wind has picked up snow, and is usually safer terrain.

- Rime, which looks like stiff white icing, on trees, rock outcrops, etc., shows us which way the wind came from.

- Clumps of snow that have fallen from trees indicate there has been wind or warming since the last snow storm.

Sleds move quickly, and good observations can easily be missed. Stop periodically to look up and around. Watch for recent avalanches, effects of wind, and past slope use. Our assessment of snow stability will be better if we collect more pieces of the puzzle. Lori Zacaruk photo.

These gullies have been cross-loaded by wind blowing from left to right. Wind has scoured snow from the ribs and deposited it in the gullies. Bruce Jamieson photo.

Wind is transporting snow from the right to the lee slope on the left. Bruce Jamieson photo.

Recent snowfall

Note accumulations of snow on parked sleds, cabins, trees, etc.

- 2 cm (1") or more per hour for a few hours will decrease snow stability substantially.

- Snowfalls of 30 cm (12") or more often require a few days to stabilize—longer if the new snow bonded poorly to the old snow, or if the air temperature has been cold.

Rain

- Rain reduces stability by adding weight to the snowpack and weakening surface layers quickly.

Air temperature

- Natural snowballs rolling down slopes indicate that surface layers are warm and weak.

- Snow becoming sticky indicates warming of snow to 0°C (32°F) and weakening of surface layers.

- Cracks that open gradually in the snow around trees indicate settlement and strengthening of

Pinwheels happen on warm days when the fresh snow surface is moist. Wet snow avalanches can occur under these same conditions. If you see only old pinwheels from a few days ago, then the snow surface has likely gained strength. Bruce Jamieson photo.

surface layers, but the strengthening is not necessarily penetrating to deeper weak layers.

- Following mild temperatures, say +5°C (23°F) or above, a cooling trend will usually improve snow stability.

Observations to note when sledding and walking on snow

- Snow beside snowmobile skis that cracks or breaks up in blocks indicates that surface layers are cohesive and "slabby".

- Sudden collapses (whumphs) or sudden cracking of the snowpack indicate unstable slab conditions.

- Deep footprints and snowmobile tracks indicate considerable soft snow is available for wind loading.

Settlement cones and cracks form gradually around trees and indicate that the recent snow is gaining strength—but deeper weak layers may persist. Bruce Jamieson photos.

Control activity for ski areas or highways

• Avalanche closures or blasting generally indicate unstable snow in the area.

Field tests

While in or near avalanche terrain, observations can be complemented by sanowpack tests, which are taught on some avalanche courses.

Before stopping to do a field test, ask yourself the following questions:

1. Is this a safe location? Remember that some of the tests, such as a test profile, may take 10 or more minutes.

2. Is the snow at this location undisturbed by avalanches, snowmobile tracks, drifting around trees, clumps of snow that have fallen off trees, etc.?

3. How well does this location represent the slopes you want to ascend, descend or cross?

Some of the more useful field tests are:

Test profile

A test profile is an observation of snow layers from a pit dug in the snowpack.

Probing the site will help determine if there are bushes or large rocks which might make the profile misleading. A profile in a safe, undisturbed location near the valley bottom will tell you the basic layering so you can test for *changes* in the snowpack as you ascend. At higher elevations where the snowpack may be quite different, additional tests or profiles are often required.

Pits for test profiles should be dug with one smooth wall across the slope and one down the slope. Dig deeper than any suspected weak layers; a metre (3') deep is often, but not always, sufficient. Several quick profiles at different locations usually provide more useful information than one detailed profile.

Some major layers will be visible on the wall of the snow pit. Strong and weak layers can be detected by poking the exposed layers by hand, by brushing, or by sliding a finger, credit card or ruler up and down through the layers and noting the changes in resistance. A compression or shovel shear test (described on the next page) is often the final part of a test profile.

Burp test (shovel tilt test)

To test for weak layers near the top of the snowpack, cut a column of snow about 30 cm (12") square. Pick up the top 30-40 cm (12-16") of the column on your shovel, tilt the shovel blade to about 15° and tap the bottom of the shovel with your hand, gently at first, then harder. Weak layers within the snow block will show up as smooth fractures.

Compression test (tap test)[13]

The compression test finds and rates the strength of weak layers. Weak layers are identified when they compress and show up on the walls of the snow column. These compressive failures are rated according to the force required. *Very easy* means the layer failed when the column was being cut. Next, place a shovel blade on top of the column. Tap 10 times with finger tips, moving your hand from the wrist; rate any failure as *easy*. Tap 10 times moving from the elbow, and rate any failure as *moderate*. Finally hit the shovel blade 10 times with open hand or fist and rate any failures as *hard*.

Present weather

The weather forecast for the day can be obtained from the newspaper, radio, TV, recorded telephone messages,

Looking and feeling for strong and weak layers in a profile. ASARC photo.

The burp test finds most weak layers in the top 30-40 cm (12-15 ") of the snowpack. Bruce Jamieson photo.

Pops and drops[13]

Sometimes the fractures in weak snowpack layers appear so suddenly they appear to "pop". Under different conditions, the weak layer collapses suddenly allowing the overlying block to "drop". Pops and drops are more closely associated with slab avalanching than fractures in a test column that appear resistant, involve a step by step squashing of a weak layer, or fractures that break with an irregular surface (not smooth).

*The character of the fracture, i.e, whether it is sudden (**pop or drop**) or not, is a better indicator of instability than the number of taps in a compression test. The same is probably also true for a burp test.*

back cut

fracture

When carefully done, the compression test can find many of the weak layers that concern recreationists, and give an indication of stability. ASARC photo.

Without any digging, you can push a probe down through the snow and feel the major layers (only). This is fast and can be done at many sites to learn how the major layers vary in depth and hardness over the terrain.

Shovel shear test[13]

This test can be done on the flats or on a slope. With good technique, the location of weak layers—even thin weak layers—can usually be found. A shovel is used to pull on a column of snow until a weak layer in the column "shears" (breaks along a smooth plane). The test works best when the layers to be tested are 5-10 cm (2-4") below the bottom of the shovel.

The force applied to the shovel that causes a weak layer to shear can be rated as either *very easy, easy, moderate* or *hard*. Unfortunately, the shovel test gives only a very rough indication of the strength of the weak layer at the test site.

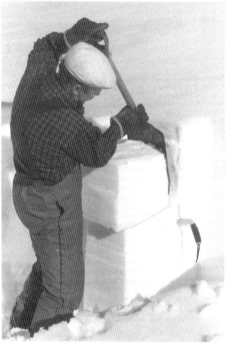

For the shovel shear test, the back wall should not be cut more than 15 cm (6") below the suspected weak layer. ASARC photo.

Slope tests

Sledders can test short slopes that are steep enough to avalanche—by highmarking them. This gives an indication of the stability of nearby larger slopes. However, as shown on the back cover, even small avalanches on short slopes have the potential to injure riders and damage sleds. Avoid slopes with terrain traps, always consider the consequences of an avalanche when you select a test slope and be aware of the positioning of the rest of your riding group. Remember, they are your rescuers should something go wrong.

Avalanches on test slopes are an indication that nearby larger slopes are probably unstable. Unfortunately, if you don't trigger an avalanche on the test slopes, it doesn't mean you cannot trigger a slide on nearby larger slopes. When assessing the avalanche danger, slope tests are only one piece of the puzzle, as discussed in this chapter.

> *The key point in snowpack tests is not the dimensions or loading stages; it is looking for smooth and/or sudden fractures.*

> *We should be a bit skeptical when interpreting block tests since they over-estimate the stability **at least** 10% of the time[14, 15, 16].*

In this test the rider traverses above the pit wall. Those below the wall—and not too close below—can watch for fractures. Kathy Burke photo.

Big block tests

There are many non-standardized big block tests that can help us find slabs overlying weak layers. Remember: the character of the fracture in the weak layer is more indicative of instability than the number of taps or the force applied to cause the fracture. Always watch for weak layers that suddenly Pop or Drop in a variety of tests. This is just part of being observant.

Yet another way to test a block...

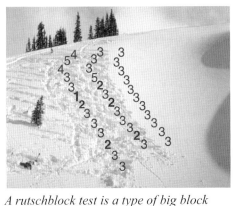

*A rutschblock test is a type of big block test in which low scores are associated with locally unstable snow. On this small slope, researchers did 36 rutschblock tests within a few hours. (The scores on the right were obtained after the photo was taken.) Clearly, the results of big block tests vary on avalanche slopes, and we must not put too much confidence on one or two high scores, which **suggest** stability. A fracture that "pops" or "drops" is a better indication of **instability** than a low test score. ASARC photo.*

No weak layers fractured. That is a good sign for this slope—but there may be a slab and weak layer on other slopes in the area. Lori Zacaruk photos.

Present weather

The weather forecast for the day can be obtained from the newspaper, radio, TV, recorded telephone messages, weather offices or information centres. Ask yourself: Will the forecasted weather tend to increase or decrease the avalanche danger?

While riding in the mountains, consider how the actual weather (as opposed to the forecasted weather) is affecting the avalanche danger and be alert for changes in weather and snow stability.

Assessing snow stability

Observations that clearly indicate unstable snow

- avalanche activity on similar slopes

- collapses or shooting cracks near the slope, or on similar slopes

Observations or test results often associated with unstable snow

Precipitation

- 2-3 cm (1") of snow per hour for two or more hours

- 30 cm (12") or more of snow within two days

- rain.

Wind

- recent or current loading of lee slopes.

Temperature

- warming the snow surface until it become sticky

Stopping to watch for changing conditions and signs of unstable snow. Lori Zacaruk photo.

- no overnight freeze.

Snowpack

- sudden fractures (pops or drops) in nearby snowpack tests.

Factors usually associated with stable snow

- a snowpack that has re-frozen after surface layers were wet

- no sudden fractures after several snowpack tests.

Unfortunately, if there is enough snow to slide, there are no conclusive signs of good stability. Also, you should be careful about using the results of such tests for slopes of different aspect, elevation or incline.

In the absence of precipitation, wind loading or deep weak layers, the following factors are usually associated with improving stability:

- obvious cooling trend especially following air temperatures near or above 0°C (32°F), or

- settlement cracks around trees.

Often the snow stability has to be assessed based on a combination of the information, observations and test results mentioned so far in this chapter.

Unfortunately, there is no simple rule or formula for combining these factors.

Experience gained from seasons of travel in avalanche terrain and from traveling with knowledgeable riders will help you make sound decisions about snow stability. Three examples at the end of this chapter illustrate the decision-making process.

If the snow is unstable, this terrain offers good options for avoiding avalanche terrain. Claude LeGroulx photo.

Terrain options

For low-risk sledding, most avalanche slopes—especially large avalanche slopes—should be avoided unless the public avalanche bulletin, field observations or field tests indicate that the local avalanche danger is low.

Sometimes, a safe alternate route may require bushwhacking or following a ridge. In some situations, the only safe alternative is to turn around.

Human factors

Many sledders are goal-oriented. Some get so focused on climbing a slope or reaching a pass, that they continue even after learning of potentially dangerous conditions! For many of us, turning around can be difficult. However, the snow slopes will still be there next weekend, and next winter.

The power of our sleds can give us a false sense of invulnerability. In fact, we are very vulnerable to avalanches because we can access so much terrain in a day.

Some accidents happen late in the day, especially when the weather is poor. Under such conditions, backcountry users often become less careful about selecting routes or observing snowpack conditions[17]. Instead, they focus on getting back to the trucks.

If we find ourselves thinking, "It won't happen to me" or "It's probably okay to cross this slope," our safety margin is too thin. The mountain snowpack continues to surprise even the most experienced riders. We need a wide margin of safety so we can continue to ride in the mountains, winter after winter.

*Blue sky draws us towards open slopes and high passes. However, a slab can remain unstable for days or sometimes weeks after the last storm. **Decisions should be based on avalanche bulletins, field observations and facts,** and not on the good feeling of being out with friends on a blue-sky day.*

Making a decision

The questions that help us recognize and reduce the local avalanche risk are:

1. Is the terrain steep enough to avalanche?

2. Is the snow stable? Often we cannot confidently answer "Yes" to this question. Hence, we must consider:

3. What is the worst that could happen on this terrain? How far could an avalanche run? Would at most one rider get caught?

The second and most difficult question is assessed using public avalanche bulletins, field observations and field tests.

Factors often neglected

An analysis of accident reports[9] shows that backcountry users have repeatedly failed to recognize the risk due to:

• terrain traps

• wind-deposited snow

• weak layers, including persistent weak layers deep in the snowpack

• sun-warmed slopes

• the possibility of triggering an avalanche from low on the slope

• the possibility of a second avalanche occurring on the same slope

Of course, we also often overlook human factors that affect our decisions.

> *Since the indications of stability are never 100% certain, we need to keep in mind the largest avalanche that we could trigger on the slope. This will help us select safe places to park while we watch the rider on the slope.*

> *If we are being swayed by human factors, e.g. "I am tired and I just want to get back to the truck", we need to tell others and make decisions based on the facts not our feelings.*

Riders parked in a safe site to watch hill climbing. Everyone should have an unobstructed escape route to an even safer area. Do not let others park in front of you. Point out to the side—away from the avalanche path. Lori Zacaruk photo.

Choosing terrain
for the current conditions

The following three pages give examples of the process of gathering regional information, making local observations and then selecting terrain within our level of acceptable risk.

Decision-making example 1

Public Avalanche Bulletin Generally *low* avalanche danger. However, slabs on lee slopes above treeline have been slower to stabilize resulting in *moderate* avalanche danger.

Recent Weather A 30 cm (12") snowfall a week ago was accompanied by moderate southwest winds. Since then winds have been light, temperatures have ranged from -15° to -5°C (5° to 23°F) and the only snowfall has been a few flurries.

Today's Weather The air temperature should rise to -10°C (14°F) during the day. Light west winds and 5 cm (2") of snow are expected.

Field Observations

- a few old fracture lines on north and northeast slopes

- some settlement cracks around trees

- snow depth at treeline is 1.5 m (4')

- snowmobile tracks at treeline are 15 cm (6") deep

Field Tests at Treeline

- compression test: a hard non-planar (irregular) *break* 20 cm (8") below the surface

Decision Southwest winds loaded lee slopes a week ago. Since then the weather has favored stabilization of the storm snow. The snowfall and west winds forecast for today will have little effect on stability provided the wind and snowfall remain light. The compression test did not find any *pops or drops* (sudden fractures).

All these factors are consistent with the *low* avalanche danger forecast below treeline. With the safety measures described in Chapter 8, we can ride below treeline or windward slopes above treeline with limited risk. However, to reduce the avalanche risk, those great-looking lee slopes in the alpine (above treeline) should either be avoided, or reassessed once we get to them. Snowpack tests can help us decide whether or not to avoid lee slopes.

Most hill climbing is in avalanche terrain, and requires a careful assessment of the avalanche danger. The loose snow avalanches in the photo are shallow, small and not the main concern. Note that wind from the left has created snow drifts and may have deposited wind slabs in the gully. Lori Zacaruk photo.

Decision-making example 2

Recent Weather It's mid-February and the winter has been generally cold. Six days ago 25 cm (10") of snow fell. Since then the weather has been cold and clear with light winds.

Today's Weather Clear skies, light winds, forecast high of -18°C (0°F).

Information from Locals The locals have been avoiding steep slopes and report numerous shooting cracks and whumphs (fractures of buried weak layers).

Field Observations Two slab avalanches apparently ran after or near the end of the storm. One small slab avalanche is visible on a northeast slope just below treeline; another larger slab has released in the alpine on a northwest-facing slope.

Field Tests At treeline, there is 90 cm (3') of snow on the ground. Snow-mobile tracks are 30 cm (12") deep. When probed, the bottom 30 cm (12") of the snowpack is noticeably weaker than the middle of the pack.

Decision Because of the cold weather, the stability of the entire snowpack including the storm snow will not be improving. The weak base and the reported collapses indicate sleds are likely to trigger slopes that are steep enough to slide. Avalanche terrain should be avoided, both above and below treeline. We should content ourselves with traveling on terrain that is not exposed to any avalanche paths, or seek alternative recreation. The public avalanche bulletin—had we remembered to call for it—reports widespread *high* avalanche danger, with some slides running on the ground.

Some days avalanche terrain is best avoided. Lori Zacaruk photo.

Often there is plenty of fresh snow when the avalanche danger is high. Take advantage of the powder snow in simple terrain and allow the slopes to stabilize. Lori Zacaruk photo.

Decision-making example 3

Recent Weather It is late March. Four days ago, a spring squall deposited 5-10 cm (2-4") in the mountains. Since then the sky has been clear, with temperatures rising to +5°C (41°F) each day and dropping to -15°C (5°F) each night. Winds have been light.

Today's Weather Sunny, warming to +8°C (46°F), winds light.

Information from Locals The snow surface becomes wet and mushy in the afternoons and then freezes into a crust each night.

Field Observations at 10:30 am Numerous wet loose slides are crashing over east-facing cliff bands. Large snowballs rolled down south-facing slopes, probably yesterday.

Field Tests A compression and a shovel test both found a hard *non-planar break* 40 cm (16") below the surface.

Decision It's spring time! We want to be leaving avalanche terrain before the corn snow that froze last night gets mushy and unstable. The sun will warm and weaken the snow on east-facing slopes first, then south-facing slopes and finally west-facing slopes. The noisy slides from the east-facing cliff bands indicate that we are probably too late for east-facing slopes. We should check south- and west-facing slopes next; hopefully we can get to them, assess their stability and—if conditions are favorable—use them before the snow surface becomes mushy.

Shady and north-facing slopes may not have experienced the same daily melting and freezing of the surface layers. Their stability may be quite different. If we are in an area with an avalanche bulletin, it may tell us what to expect on north-facing slopes. Field observations and perhaps snowpack tests will also help us decide about north-facing slopes.

There is no powder cloud from this avalanche pouring over a cliff because it is a wet avalanche on a spring afternoon. On warm spring days, be alert for avalanches from the slopes above that are exposed to the sun. Bruce Jamieson photo.

On spring mornings when the snow is frozen hard, avalanches are unlikely and we can ride fast. But we need to head back before the surface snow gets mushy, weak and prone to avalanching. Lori Zacaruk photo.

Canadian Supplement to Chapter 6

The challenge

It is really difficult to interpret the various local snow and weather observations along with the regional bulletin and make decisions about which terrain is low risk under the current conditions. It can take decades to get good at this! However, there are rule-based methods, first developed in Europe, that provide an optional aid for selecting terrain based on the current bulletin and local conditions. These methods can help us avoid the human factors that can compromse decisions.

The Avaluator[18]

The Avaluator is a pocket card that was developed by the Canadian Avalanche Centre to help Canadian backcountry users make decisions about which terrain to access when.

There are four main steps in making decisions:

1. trip planning (Chapter 6, 9)

2. identifying avalanche terrain (Chapter 4)

3. evaluating specific slopes (Chapter 6), and

4. practicing good travel habits (Chapter 7)

One side of the Avaluator pocket card helps with *trip planning* and the other side can help people consider some of the most important factors for *specific slopes.*

The Avaluator does not forecast avalanches or predict risk. It does, however, offer a consistent method for combining observations—including the bulletin—and compares some important factors about the current situation with those same factors in previous avalanche accidents.

The card and accompanying booklet include professional suggestions about the training and experience for travel under various conditions.

There is more information on the Avaluator at www.avalanche.ca. The use of the Avaluator is taught in Avalanche Skills Training 1 (AST 1) courses, which are available in many Canadian communities.

Chapter 7
Good Riding Habits

Safety equipment

Every rider in avalanche terrain should have a beacon, probe and shovel. The beacon should be worn under outer clothing, where it will be warm and less likely to get torn off by an avalanche. The probe and shovel should be in the pack on your back.

The group should also have

- first aid kit
- repair kit
- extra food
- extra warm clothing
- foam pad and "bivy" sack (sleeping bag cover)
- map, compass and GPS receiver
- a cell phone if there is coverage. A satellite phone is also a good option.

Appendix E contains a checklist for a day trip.

Trip preparation

Route plan

Whenever practical, make a plan that includes alternate routes and play areas to give your group options should the snow stability or weather deteriorate.

Create trips that avoid terrain features such as glaciers and ridge tops which are prone to 'whiteouts' and high winds.

Balloon packs do not replace beacons. However, if you are wearing a balloon pack and trigggger it when an avalanche approaches, the odds of you being found on the surface—and alive—are good. The balloons are triggered by a handle on the shoulder strap, and inflate in a couple of seconds. Lori Zacaruk photo.

Keep your shovel and probe in your pack on your back. That way, you have it when you get separated from your sled, which happens in avalanches and during rescues.

The best time to ensure you have all the gear is before you leave. Randy Zacaruk photo.

Be prepared to camp out on any riding day. Damaged sleds, injured and lost riders and serious weather changes have caused many snowmobilers to spend an uncomfortable night out in the bush.

Local information

Ask locals about access routes, travel conditions, the snowpack, weather trends, and avalanche activity. Then go and see for yourself. First-hand information is always better than second-hand information.

Public forecasts and bulletins

Weather and avalanche forecasts are invaluable and can be obtained from the media, recorded telephone messages or the internet.

Group compatibility

Some sledders like long, demanding tours; others prefer aggressive high-marking; and still others enjoy a more leisurely pace. If riders with these various expectations are mixed in the same group, the group will often split up. It is far better to agree on the pace and expectations when planning the trip. Factors that affect pace include fitness, experience and type of sled.

Trip planning: Reducing the avalanche risk starts at home with the avalanche bulletin, weather forecast, terrain information and selecting your group. Bruce Jamieson photo.

Leadership

Many people prefer to travel in groups of peers without a designated leader. In such situations, the entire group should be involved in assessing the avalanche danger and selecting appropriate route and slopes.

Perform a beacon check to confirm that all units are properly receiving and transmitting before you leave the staging area. Also, re-check that all units are transmitting after a rescue exercise. Lori Zacaruk photo.

However, in difficult situations such as an avalanche rescue, a group with a leader will function better than a group without a leader. Some good leaders will only take charge in difficult situations.

Group safety

Give a responsible friend a copy of your trip plan, noting the location you plan to park and your truck's license plate number.

Be sure you know who will bring each item of group and safety equipment and then, just before the trip starts, check that no equipment has been forgotten.

Each morning at the motel, turn on your beacon to check its batteries. At the staging area, check that everyone can receive and transmit. Large groups should bring a spare beacon.

It's advantageous to start each day of your trip early and plan to finish early. That way a broken sled or other setback is less likely to lead to travel after dark.

A surprising number of accidents happen when members of a group are out of visual contact.

Sometimes a quiet voice asking, "But why do we think that slope won't slide?" can prompt a careful re-assessment of the avalanche danger and, ultimately, a sound decision.

Also, people "back in the pack" may just follow the track, paying little attention to the terrain or snowpack.

To keep your party together, position a proficient rider with tools, a strong back and good knowledge of the area at the back of a large group.

Route selection

The following factors are helpful in selecting good routes:

- Wind-scoured slopes are generally safer than wind-loaded slopes.

- Broad valley bottoms are usually safer than the surrounding slopes; but keep in mind that large avalanches can run well across valley bottoms and sometimes start up the other side of the valley.

- Dense timber is usually considered safe[20] but sledding is often difficult or impractical in dense timber.

- Narrow ridges are usually safe from avalanches but there may be a hazard from wind, cornices or the steep slopes beside the ridge.

- If there is no way to avoid a slope of doubtful stability, it should be crossed as high as possible.

- In particular, convex portions of slopes should be avoided if you are concerned about the avalanche danger.

Although this list of route-finding basics is a useful start, we continue to learn the many subtleties of route selection as long as we ride in the mountains. Traveling with experienced riders is a great way to hone route-finding skills, especially if route selection is discussed within the group.

These sledders are discussing potential routes down and the safe areas for them to group up. Usually, more than one option should be discussed before picking the best one. Lori Zacaruk photo.

Many people are injured or killed in situations they know to be dangerous. We must not let our desire to reach a pass or climb a perfect slope to override our assessment of the danger.

Sledding in avalanche terrain

Even after you have decided to run up or down a particular slope, the following precautions help reduce the avalanche risk:

- Go one at a time.

- Plan your route, your escape route, and who will go first and last.

- When not riding, move to a safe place where you can watch the others in your group.

- Go where the snow is deepest, avoiding areas where the slab may be thin and easily triggered[10].

- Stay in visual contact. Look back to check that you are not getting too far ahead of the rider behind you.

- When hill climbing, turn out early so you don't get stuck.

Turning out early when hill climbing means you are unlikely to get stuck, which is easier on your back. It also reduces the load on the slope and the number of people exposed to danger. As well, it reduces the temptation for those waiting at the bottom to run the slope as their patience wears thin.

Sometimes, broad valley bottoms offer low-risk access routes. Lori Zacaruk photo.

Crossing or climbing a possibly unstable slope

If possible, find a safer route.

- Choose escape routes before entering the slope.

- Fasten your clothing so it, and your beacon, are less less likely to get torn off in an avalanche.

- Travel quickly one at a time between islands of safety. Persons in safe places should observe those exposed to the hazard.

- If an avalanche approaches, call out to observers and try to ride to safety, usually to the side of the avalanche.

Cornices, like the one on the right, have broken off farther back than many experienced sledders expected. Best to stay well back as shown here.Lori Zacaruk photo.

One rider watches another from a safe distance. Lori Zacaruk photo.

> *If a fellow rider gets stuck on an avalanche slope, e.g. while hill climbing, do NOT go to help. Avalanches have been triggered too often when one rider goes to help another.*

Too often, avalanches have been triggered when one rider goes to help another. Jamon Ludwar photo.

Pulling the trigger on the shoulder strap of a balloon pack.

If you cannot ride your sled out of the avalanche

- Trigger your balloon pack if you are wearing one.

- Jump off, or push away from your sled to avoid being injured by it.

- Fight to get towards the side of the avalanche.

- Swim or struggle to stay on the surface of the avalanche.

- Grab trees, rocks, etc.

- Keep your mouth shut.

Inflating...

When the avalanche slows

- Make a strong thrust towards the surface[4].

- Make an air space in front of your face with your hands and forearms. The bigger the air space the more time searchers will have to find you alive. (Sometimes visors seem to create air spaces, sometimes they are packed with snow.)

Fully inflated, within a few seconds! ASARC photos.

When the avalanche stops

- Make an initial attempt to dig yourself out.

- Then, if buried, try to relax your breathing and stay calm.

- Shout only when a searcher is near.

Waiting for someone? Any safe area is a good place to practise searching with a beacon. Randy Zacaruk photo.

Before climbing big hills, gather many puzzle pieces as you can to get a good indication of the snow stability. Slope tests are one type of puzzle piece. Start on small steep slopes to check the reaction of the snow. If your stability observations look good, work your way up to larger slopes. This slope is large enough to bury a rider and machine; however, it is free of terrain traps and there is plenty of safe area for your partners to maintain visual contact. Lori Zacaruk photo.

How far back is safe?

Darcy Svederus

April 4, 2004   14:30 hours
Location: Blackwater/Renshaw near
        McBride, BC
Altitude: 6200 ft., *Aspect:* west
Weather: clear and calm, 6 C
Average crown: 1 metre
Sliding layer: facets

This close call where no-one was caught or injured occurred when one of the guys in our group was high marking approximately 1.5 km north of where I was. I had 3 beacons buried around my sled. (The Ski-doo). The guys were taking turns at the slope one at a time when I heard something like a wine bottle pop. I looked up to where one of the guys was just turning out and I could see the fracture line just starting to appear above where he was turning out. The slab at first was about the size of two football fields. I remember thinking the guy on this slab doesn't even know yet. After moving about 50 meters down slope the slab started breaking up. The rider was now fully aware and was able to accelerate off the slab that was picking up speed.

I was watching this from over a kilometre away and when the initial avalanche had come down slope about 500 meter, we heard two more sounds like wine bottles popping. We looked up above and could see fractures appearing from where the first one had started all the way across the top of the slope past where we were practicing with beacons. In my opinion, we were in a SAFE area and the slide would never reach us. The avalanche seemed to be in slow motion. I was mesmerised by the colour of the churning snow which was deep blue. 20 km/h was probably the fastest it was traveling and I was thinking "it will never reach us", but it kept coming. The further it came down slope the deeper it became. When it finally came to a stop, it was 1 km long, over 8 ft deep and 10 ft. from the bumper of my sled. I was in a safe area, **but not safe enough**. Yes, I had abandoned my sled.

I really feel the biggest lesson learned that day, for myself and the others in the group, was just because the avalanche was slow moving doesn't mean that our reactions should be slow as well. In these instances, slow can also have very serious consequences. We all learned that day that even slow moving avalanches can cover **great** distances and pack a huge punch.

ALWAYS BE SURE OF YOUR SAFE AREAS!

Chapter 8
Search and Rescue

The time for live rescue is short

Approximately 25% of avalanche victims are fatally injured by the motion of the avalanche or collisions with the ground, trees or rocks[2,3]. An additional 25% die from suffocation in the next 30 minutes. Therefore, to have a 50% chance of saving someone who has been buried by an avalanche, that person should be found and dug out within half an hour.

> *In most backcountry situations, if you go out to get help from an organized or professional rescue group, there is little chance the buried person(s) will still be alive when the rescue group arrives at the avalanche.* **Companion rescue is by far the victim's best chance for survival.**

Companion rescue

If you see the avalanche

- Ensure your personal safety.
- Watch the victim and note the last seen point.

Before you enter the slope

- Be calm and methodical.

- Appoint a leader.

- Note who is missing.

- Assess further danger, and post an avalanche guard in a safe place if necessary.

- Ensure everyone knows where to run if another avalanche occurs.

- If your group is large, designate shovelers.

> *The visual search for surface clues should start **before** the beacon search or any probing.*

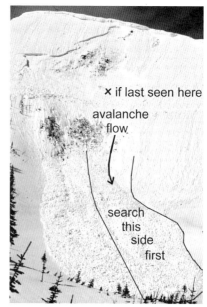

× if last seen here

avalanche flow

search this side first

Search in the most like burial areas first. This includes major deposits below the last seen point and in line with the victim's sled or other articles. Bruce Jamieson photo.

- Leave snowmobiles, gasoline and heavy, unnecessary items away from the search area.

- Designate who will enter the slope and physically check that **all** the beacons are switched to receive.

When you enter the slope

- If practical, mark the *last seen point* with a branch, etc.

- Look for the victim's sled, articles, hands or boots sticking out of snow. Check or pull on these first to see if the victim is with the article, but do not remove the items from the deposit.

- Focus the initial search on major deposits below the last seen point and in line with the victim's sled or other visual clues.

- Don't leave your helmet, gloves, etc., on the slope.

- Don't spit or urinate on the slope. (Either could distract an avalanche dog.)

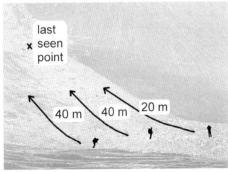

*If the deposit is wide and there are multiple searchers for the **signal search**, they should start about 40 m apart (120') and about 20 m (60') from the side of the deposit. Bruce Jamieson photo,*

Beacon search

A beacon search is appropriate if at least one searcher and one buried victim have beacons (transceivers). There are digital beacons which show decreasing numbers (distance) as the searcher gets closer to the transmitting beacon. There are analogue transceivers which beep louder or flash more lights as the searcher gets closer to the buried transmitter. Some have a combination of these features.

- Select a *signal search* pattern and a number of beacon searchers, e.g. 40 m apart as shown in the photo, that suits the size of the deposit is below the *last seen point*.

- Move quickly. When you pick up a signal, call out "Signal" to let the other searchers know you are leaving the signal search and starting the coarse search pattern.

- Use the methods recommended by the manufacturer of the beacon to home in and pin-point the victim's signal.

- Gently probe the victim and leave the probe in place while shoveling.

- Give the victim first aid and switch their beacon to receive.

- When the last victim is uncovered, ensure all beacons are transmitting.

- If your group has a radio or cell phone and you require help to evacuate the victim, call for assistance.

Coarse search using the induction line method

1. While holding the beacon pointing ahead of you, turn your body and the beacon to get the strongest signal (lowest distance number, maximum volume or most lights).

2. If possible, turn down the volume so the beep is audible but not loud.

3. Walk about 5 m (15'). If the signal gets weaker, walk 10 m (30') in the opposite direction.

4. While holding the beacon in front of you, turn your body to get the strongest signal. Turn the volume down if practical. Walk 5 m (15') in the direction the beacon is pointing.

5. Repeat step 4. As the signal gets stronger, slow down and reduce the number of steps between stops to re-orientate the beacon.

6. When the distance number drops below 3-5 or moving does not change the volume much (on the lowest or second lowest setting). start the pin-point search.

Move quickly over the deposit and home in on the victim's signal. If two searchers are homing in on one signal, one of them can prepare a probe and shovel for the next stage of the rescue. Bruce Jamieson photo.

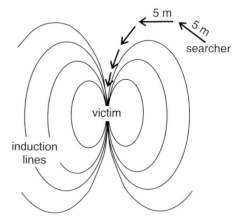

All avalanche beacons transmit in this egg-shaped pattern. Searchers can follow an induction line to get close to the buried transmitter. As you home in on the signal, slow down and re-orient the receiver more often.

Fine search (pin-pointing)

1. Loosen the strap or remove the beacon so you can hold the beacon close to the snow.

2. Move your beacon along a straight line (mini-bracket) by moving your feet, instead of just reaching with the beacon. Find the strongest signal along the mini-bracket. Turn down the volume if practical.

3. From the point with the strongest signal, do another mini-bracket at 90° to the previous one.

4. Repeat the mini-brackets until the strongest signal in any direction has been located.

5. Gently probe to locate the person and start shoveling.

During the fine search (pin-pointing), try to hold the beacon a constant height above the snow. Lori Zacaruk collection.

The searcher on the right is pin-pointing the signal. The searcher on the left is ready with the probe and shovel, but should not crowd the beacon searcher. Lori Zacaruk photo.

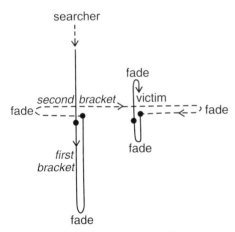

A bracket extends in a straight line between two points where the signal fades. After finishing a bracket, return to the middle where the signal is strong (and turn down the volume if possible) before starting the next bracket.

Searching for multiple signals

- If your beacon indicates more than one signal while searching, focus your attention on one pattern of beeps while you search. Each buried transmitter will have a distinct patterns of beeps.

- If you appear to be converging on the same signal as another searcher, back away and try to pick up another signal.

- There are various methods of searching for multiple signals that are taught on courses. Different methods may be suited to different models of beacons. The micro search strip is one method.

The micro search strip

- To avoid missing a victim when more than one is buried in a small area, use a square search pattern, advancing about 2.5 m (8').

- When you get a strong signal, pinpoint the signal, probe then shovel out the victim. Turn their beacon off if practical.

- Continue the search until all buried people in the area have been found.

Probe search

Compared to a beacon search, a probe search is very, very slow. Probe lines find bodies more often than live victims.

Specially designed probes work best but people have been found by probing with poles and branches.

- If your group has a radio, cell or satellite phone, call for help.

- Ensure searchers have their beacons on transmit.

- Identify likely burial areas in line with avalanche flow from the last seen point.

- Spot-probe (without using a line of probers) any small, likely deposits.

- If the spot-probing is unsuccessful, set up a line of probers (or two), again considering the last seen point and estimated trajectory. Work quickly.

> *Many buried riders are found near their sleds, so that's a good place to start spot probing.*

Probing for a buried victim. Lori Zacaruk photo.

Probe line with two holes per step[19]

- If the transceiver search is complete, ensure probers have their beacons on transmit.

- Probers should stand with extended arms, touching wrists, about 1.5 metres (5 feet) apart.

- The probemaster coordinates the probe line with the commands "Probe" and "Step".

- The probemaster should be on one end of the line, probing with the others and setting a pace that can be maintained.

Two holes per step probing

wrist to wrist apart

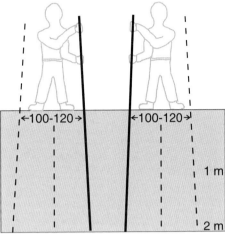

For two hole per step probing, probe vertically to the left and right and then step ahead. Try to maintain wrist to wrist spacing.

- On the command "Probe," reach the probe about 38 centimetres (15 inches) to the left of your mid-chest and push the probe down vertically. Then remove it.

- Repeat 38 centimetres (15 inches) to the right of your mid-chest.

- On the command "Step," move forward 70 centimetres (28 inches).

- If your probe encounters any soft or suspicious objects, leave it in the snow. If additional (gentle) probing confirms the possible presence of a victim, then begin shoveling.

- If possible, use flagging or wands to mark probed areas.

- After probing all deposits below the last seen point, either do it again or send for organized help.

Three holes per step probing

fingertip to fingertip apart

*After probing between your feet, to the left and to the right, step forward 70 cm (28"). When probing to the left or right, do not try for a certain angle. Rather, probe **as close to vertical as practical** to avoid missing a buried victim. Try to maintain fingertip to fingertip spacing.*

Probe line with three holes per step[6, 19]

This alternative probing technique searches the deposit faster than traditional techniques but requires more practice.

- Probers should stand finger-tip-to-fingertip apart, about 175 cm (70").

- The probemaster should be on one end of the line, probing with the others and setting a pace that can be maintained.

- The probemaster coordinates the probe line with the commands "Probes down" and "Step forward."

- On the command "Probes down," push the probe down between your feet and remove it. Reach to your left and push the probe, *as close to vertical as practical*, into the snow 50-60 cm (20-24") to the left of the first hole. Repeat 50-60 cm to the right of the first hole.

- Step forward 70 cm (28").

- If your probe encounters any soft or suspicious objects, leave it in the snow. If additional (gentle) probing confirms the possible presence of a victim, then begin shoveling.

- If practical, use flagging or wands to mark probed areas.

- After probing all deposits below the last seen point, either do it again or send for organized help.

> *To have the best chance of finding someone alive with a probe line, work quickly. The probing for a body a day later should be slower and more precise; often the pattern of holes is finer.*

Leave the probe in place and shovel quickly. Start shoveling the hole on the downhill side of the victim. This won't collapse any air space near the victim's face, and is more efficient. Lori Zacaruk photo.

Shoveling

Dig a hole on the downhill side of the probe. Start the hole about 1.5 times as long as the victim is buried[20], and about 1.5 m (5') wide. In a dense deposit, cut snow into blocks before shoveling the blocks out of the pit.

Going for organized help

- Don't rush off.

- Write the accident situation and the group's needs on paper (Appendix F).

- Mark the accident location, a suitable location for a helicopter to land, and a proposed route on a map.

- Plan the trip, and take ample supplies.

- If possible, don't travel alone.

Organized rescue

An organized avalanche rescue party will typically include a helicopter, a trained avalanche dog, advanced first aid equipment and—most importantly—the people trained to use these resources.

Before the helicopter lands, pack the landing area with your sleds, secure light objects, stay well back from the landing site, put on your helmet and lower your visor. Approach the helicopter on foot only when directed by the pilot and then crouch while approaching from the front (or front downhill side), making sure the pilot can see you.

As a member of the accident party, you should:

- provide information about the accident such as last seen point, number of people missing and which victims had beacons,

- tell the person in charge how you feel (cold, exhausted, etc.),

- assist the rescue team if you are asked.

Pack the landing site with your sleds. Stay well back from the landing site and secure loose objects when the helicopter approaches. Lori Zacaruk photo.

In this avalanche, a rider and his sled were buried. The rider was buried face down, and soon passed out. The rescuers used beacons and probes to find him. He was was not breathing when they dug him out but they were able to revive him. The dense snow packed around his sled is typical of the snow packed around the faces of many victims. This is the main reason why companion rescues must be efficient. Alan Harder photo.

Stages of Companion Search

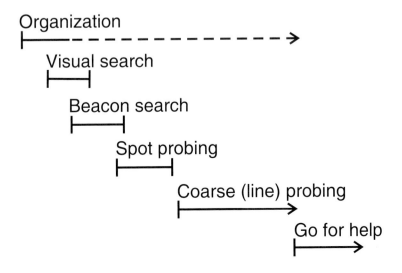

Organization

Visual search

Beacon search

Spot probing

Coarse (line) probing

Go for help

Chapter 9
Key Points for Reducing the Risk
These two pages can be photocopied and carried with you.

Before you go

Get current weather and avalanche information (See www.avalanche.ca or www.avalanche.org for links and phone numbers).

Select a desintation that includes some non-avalanche terrain—especially if the avalanche danger is rated as considerable or higher.

Select riders who

- choose a level of risk you are comfortable with,
- are equipped with avalanche beacons, shovels and probes,
- know how to use their rescue gear, and
- if possible, know the area and the avalanche slopes in the area.

Check that your avalanche beacons are working wherever you gear up—before you get to the trailhead.

Always be observant and share what you observe with your fellow riders. This very small slab avalanche indicates a deep week layer and the potential for large slab avalanches. Bruce Jamieson photo.

On the way to the staging area

Watch for

- avalanches on the slopes visible from the road,
- highway closures for avalanche control, and
- snowfall, rain, or blowing snow.

Some signs to watch for while riding

Regardless of the regional danger rating, if you see fresh avalanches or shooting cracks in the snow, or hear "whumpf" sounds, the local avalanche danger may be *high* or *extreme*. Also, the avalanche danger is probably increasing if you see

- heavy snowfall,
- rain,
- blowing snow, or
- the snow surface becoming wet or sticky.

Choosing routes and slopes

Discuss the route and slopes with the group. Include all riders in the discussion since less vocal riders may be good at assessing the avalanche danger and, if not, will learn from the discussion.

Avalanches usually start on slopes over 35°, rarely on slopes under 25°.

Windward slopes (that face the recent wind) are usually safer than leeward slopes (that face down-wind). Cornices sometimes form at the top of leeward slopes.

If one slope has avalanched recently, others that face the same way are often unstable.

Watch for signs of the snow surface warming to the melting point, such as sticky snow or pinwheeling.

Terrain traps increase the danger of particular slopes. They include gullies or creeks in which you might get buried deeply, or cliffs that you might get carried over.

Good riding habits

If you think a slope is dangerous, avoid it if practical, or cross it one at a time.

Watch your fellow sledders while they are riding on, or below, an avalanche slope.

Don't stop in areas exposed to avalanches, even to watch hill climbing.

Climb one at time and watch from a safe place. Lori Zacaruk photo.

Even if you think you are stopping far enough away from an avalanche slope, park beside—not behind—other sleds. Point your sled towards a completely safe area, and keep your kill switch up, ready for a quick departure.

Most good slopes for hill-climbing are avalanche slopes. If you choose to climb, go one at a time. Do not go up to help a rider with a stuck sled.

If an avalanche releases, try to ride to either side, out of its path.

If you are caught in an avalanche, push away from your sled. Keep your mouth shut. Grab trees or rocks—maybe the avalanche will leave you behind. Fight to get to the side of the avalanche, or struggle to stay on the surface of the avalanche.

As the avalanche slows, use both hands to make an air space in front of your face.

Rescue

Pick a leader. *Switch all beacons to receive and then check them!*

Focus the search below the point where the victim was last seen.

Search the avalanche deposit visually for hands, gloves, boots, etc., then search with beacons for completely buried victims.

When a beacon searcher is as close to the victim as practical, probe for the victim. Leave the probe in place and start shoveling.

Start first aid as soon as the victim's face is exposed.

Books, Videos and References

Some good reading

Books available at some mountain shops or over the internet:

Staying Alive in Avalanche Terrain. Bruce Tremper. (The Mountaineers, Seattle), 284 pp.

Snow Sense: A Guide to Evaluating Avalanche Hazards, third edition, by J.A. Fredston and D. Fesler. 1988. (Alaska Mountain Safety Center, Anchorage), 48 pp.

Avalanche Accidents in Canada, Volume 4: 1984-96. B. Jamieson and T. Geldsetzer. 1996. (Canadian Avalanche Association, P.O. Box 2759, Revelstoke, BC, V0E 2S0), 202 pp.

The Avalanche Handbook, by D.M. McClung and P.A. Schaerer. 2006. (The Mountaineers, Seattle), 342 pp.

The Avalanche Book, revised edition, by B.R. Armstrong and K. Williams. 1992. (Colorado Geological Survey, Denver, CO), 240 pp.

The ABCs of Avalanche Safety, third edition by S.A. Ferguson and E.R. LaChapelle, 2003. (The Mountaineers, Seattle), 192 pp.

The Snowy Torrents - Avalanche Accidents in the United States 1980-86, by N. Logan and D. Atkins. 1996. (Colorado Geological Survey, Special Publication 39), 275 pp.

And some videos

Riding Safely in Avalanche Country, about 30 minutes. Contact http://www.avalanche.org or nac@sunvalley.net.

Rules of the Snow - Snowmobiling Safety Video, 50 minutes. SavaFilm, Box 836, Wilson, WY 83014. http://www.savafilm.com

Beating the Odds, 30 minutes. Canadian Avalanche Association, PO Box 2759, Revelstoke, BC, V0E 2S0. Phone 1-250-837-2435. http://www.avalanche.ca

Winning the Avalanche Game, 58 minutes. Friends of the Utah Avalanche Forecast Center, http://www.avalanche.org/~uac/ed-bookvideo-m.htm.

Know Before You Go, 15 minutes. Friends of the Utah Avalanche Centre, http://www.avalanche.org/~uac/ed-kbyg.htm

References

1. Avalanche incident data from Westwide Avalanche Network (www. avalanche.org) and Cyberspace Snow and Avalanche Centre (www.csac.org), obtained August 2007.

2. B. Jamieson and T. Geldsetzer. 1996. Avalanche Accidents in Canada, Vol. 4: 1984-96. (Canadian Avalanche Association, PO Box 2759, Revelstoke, BC, V0E 2S0), 202 pp.

3. Bruce Tremper. Staying Alive in Avalanche Terrain. (The Mountaineers, Seattle), 284 pp.

4. P.A. Schaerer. 1988. Studies on survival in avalanches. Canadian Alpine Journal 71, 55-56.

5. P.A. Schaerer. 1981. Avalanches in: Handbook of Snow, Eds. D.M. Gray and D.H. Male (Pergamon Press, Toronto), 475-518.

6. D.M. McClung and P.A. Schaerer. 2006. The Avalanche Handbook, second edition. (The Mountaineers, Seattle), 342 pp.

7. R.I. Perla. 1977. Slab avalanche measurements. Canadian Geotechnical Journal 14(2), 206-213.

8. S.A. Ferguson and E.R. LaChapelle. 2003. The ABCs of Avalanche Safety, third edition, (The Mountaineers, Seattle), 192 pp.

9. P.A. Schaerer. 1987. Avalanche Accidents in Canada III. A Selection of Case Histories 1978-1984. (National Research Council of Canada, no. 27950), 183 pp.

10. N. Logan. 1993. Snow temperature patterns and artificial avalanche release. Proceedings of the 1992 International Snow Science Workshop in Breckenridge. (Colorado Avalanche Information Center, Denver, CO), 37-46.

11. G. Statham, B. McMahon and I. Tomm. 2006. The avalanche terrain exposure scale. (A. Gleason, ed.) Proceedings of the 2006 International Snow Science Workshop in Telluride, Colorado, USA., 491-497.

12. B. Jamieson and C.D. Johnston. 1992. Snowpack characteristics associated with avalanche accidents. Canadian Geotechnical Journal 29, 862-866.

13. Canadian Avalanche Association. 2007. Observation Guidelines and Recording Standards for Weather, Snowpack and Avalanche Observations. (Canadian Avalanche Association, PO Box 2759, Revelstoke, BC V0E 2S0), 85 pp.

14. B. Jamieson. 1999. The compression test - after 25 years. The Avalanche Review 18(1), 10-12.

15. P.M.B. Föhn. 1987. The 'rutschblock' as a practical tool for slope stability evaluation in: Avalanche Formation, Movement and Effects, Eds. B. Salm and H. Gubler. IAHS publication 162, 223-228.

16. B. Jamieson and C. Johnston. 1995. Interpreting rutschblocks in avalanche start zones. Avalanche News, 46, 2-4.

17. J. Fredston, D. Fesler and B. Tremper. 1995. The human factor - lessons for avalanche education. Proceedings of the International Snow Science Workshop at Snowbird, International Snow Science Workshop 1994, (PO Box 49, Snowbird, Utah 84092, USA), 473-486.

18. P. Haegeli and I. McCammon. 2006. Avaluator Avalanche Accident Prevention Card. Canadian Avalanche Centre, Revelstoke, BC, Canada

19. T. Auger and B. Jamieson. 1996. Avalanche probing revisited. Proceedings of the October 1996 International Snow Science Workshop in Banff, 295-298. (Canadian Avalanche Association, PO Box 2759, Revelstoke, V0E 2S0,

Appendix A Glossary

Avalanche cycle - A period of avalanches associated with a storm or warm weather. For snow storms, the cycle typically starts during the storm and ends a few days after the storm.

Avalanche beacon (transceiver) - An electronic device worn by people in avalanche terrain. In transmit mode, it constantly transmits a radio signal which is stronger at closer range. If someone with a transmitting transceiver is buried, the other members of the group can switch their transceivers into receive mode and follow a search pattern that locates the strongest signal. The person is then found by probing and shovelling.

Bed surface - The surface on which an avalanche runs. Not to be confused with failure plane (see failure plane).

Cornice - An overhanging build-up of snow, usually on the lee side of ridges. Moderate or strong winds often create a vortex on the lee side and deposit wind-blown snow at the very top of the lee slope. Cornices generally form faster during periods of high humidity.

Cross-loaded - When wind blows across a cross-loaded slope, snow is picked up from the windward side of ribs and outcrops and is deposited in lee pockets.

Depth hoar - An advanced, generally larger, form of faceted crystal (see facets). Depth hoar crystals are striated and, in later stages, often form hollow shapes. Cup-shaped crystals are a common form of depth hoar. This type of crystal can form at any level in the snowpack but is most commonly found at the base of shallow snowpacks following periods of cold weather.

Failure plane - The fracture that releases a slab avalanche spreads along a weak snowpack layer called the failure plane. The bed surface usually lies immediately below the failure plane.

Facets (also called faceted crystals or sometimes *sugar snow*) - In response to a sufficiently strong temperature gradient within the snowpack, grains grow flat faces by a process know as *kinetic growth* or simply *faceting*. Facets commonly form near the snow surface or where the snowpack is shallow during periods of cold weather.

Hill climbing - The activity in which snowmobilers drive up a steep slope, each trying to reach a higher point than the previous rider. When the sled slows at the top of the run, the rider turns down the slope.

Melt-freeze crust - A layer of snow that has been warmed until liquid water forms between the grains and then freezes to form a relatively strong layer. Crusts sometimes form the *bed surface* for slab avalanches.

Propagation - The spreading of a fracture or crack. The shear fractures that spread along weak snow layers and release slab avalanches tend to propagate further under thicker, harder slabs than under thinner, softer slabs.

Rime - A deposit of ice from super-cooled water droplets. Rime can accumulate on the windward side of rocks, trees or structures, or on falling crystals of snow. When snow crystals cannot be recognised because of rime, the grains are called *graupel*.

Rounded grains (rounds) - Under sufficiently low *temperature gradients*, branched and angular crystals decompose into more rounded shapes called rounds. This dry-snow process involves the sublimation of ice from convex parts of grains into hollows. Rounding also tends to build bonds between grains (*sintering*). Consequently, layers of rounded grains are often stronger than layers of faceted grains of similar density.

Slab - One or more cohesive layers of snow that may start to slide together.

Sluff - A small avalanche usually made up of loose snow.

Stepped down - A slab avalanche is said to step down if the motion of the initial slab causes lower layers to slide, resul-ting in a second bed surface deeper in the snowpack. A step in the bed surface is usually visible.

Storm snow - The snow that falls during a period of continuous or almost continuous snowfall. Many operations consider a storm to be over after a day with less than 1 cm of snow.

Sun crust - The term *sun crust* is often used to refer to a melt-freeze crust that is more noticeable on sunny slopes than on shady slopes. However, the international definition[13] is a thin, transparent layer (also called *firnspiegel*) caused by partial melting and refreezing of the surface layer.

Surface hoar - Crystals, often shaped like feathers, spikes or wedges, that grow upward from the snow surface when air just above the snow surface is cooled to the dew point. The winter equivalent of dew. Surface hoar grows most often when the wind is calm or light on cold, relatively clear nights. These crystals can also grow during the day on shady slopes. Once buried, layers of surface hoar are slow to gain strength, sometimes persisting for a month or more as potential failure planes for slab avalanches.

Temperature gradient - The temperature gradient is the change in temperature with depth in the snowpack. For example, if the temperature 20 cm below the surface is 3° warmer than the surface, then the temperature gradient in the top 20 cm averages 1.5° per 10 cm. Gradients greater than 1° per 10 cm are often associated with faceting of crystals and weakening of layers, whereas lower gradients are usually associated with rounding of grains and strengthening of layers. However, the transition between faceting and rounding also depends on factors other than the temperature gradient.

Terrain trap - A terrain feature that increases the consequences of getting caught in an avalanche. For example, gullies and crevasses increase the odds of a deep burial, and cliffs increase the odds of traumatic injuries.

Whumpf - The sound of a fracture propagating along a weak layer within the snowpack. Whumpfs are indicators of local instability. In terrain steep enough to avalanche, whumpfs usually result in slab avalanches.

Wind-loaded - Terrain on which the wind has deposited additional snow. Slopes on the lee sides of ridges are often wind-loaded.

Wind-slab - One or more stiff layers of wind-deposited snow. Wind slabs usually consist of snow crystals broken into small particles by the wind and packed together.

Appendix B
Snow Metamorphism

Dry Snow Metamorphism

There are two metamorphic processes in dry snow: rounding and faceting.

Rounding

In the rounding process (previously called equi-temperature or ET metamorphism) the grains become more blob-shaped and bond to neighboring grains. Part way through this process, when the original shapes of the new snow crystals can still be identified under a hand-held magnifier, the grains are called *partly decomposed* or *partly settled*. Because of the bonding between grains, **as the grains in a layer become rounder, the layers of these grains become progressively stronger.** During the rounding process, a snow layer will become denser and, over a period of days, settlement of the layer is often noticeable.

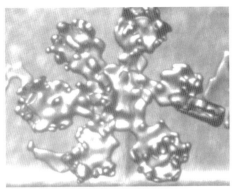

This stellar crystal has changed a little since it fell from the sky. The small balls of ice are rime—supercooled droplets that froze onto the crystal as it fell. Chris Stethem photo.

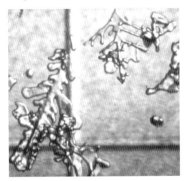

These pieces of stellar crystals are considered partly decomposed particles. Chris Stethem photo.

Rounding
(common in thick snowpack)

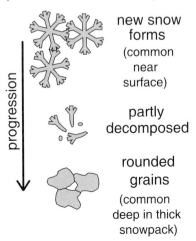

progression

new snow forms
(common near surface)

partly decomposed

rounded grains
(common deep in thick snowpack)

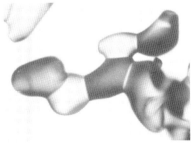

These rounded grains bear no resemblance to the original new snow forms. Note the large bonds. Ron Perla photo.

Faceting

In the faceting process, also called recrystallization or temperature gradient (TG) metamorphism, ice is deposited on the grains by the flow of water vapor through the snow. (Usually, the flow of water vapor is upwards and the ice is deposited on the bottom surfaces of the grains.) These deposits are first noticeable as corners on the grains and then as completely flat surfaces called *facets*. If the process continues, the grains will grow and take on a layered or stepped appearance. The final product of the process is an often-fragile layer consisting of large *depth hoar* grains. One of the most common forms of depth hoar is a hollow, cup-shaped grain. Depth hoar occurs most commonly at the bottom of thin snowpacks.

In contrast to rounding, which bonds grains together and strengthens layers, **faceting usually forms few bonds between the grains and progressive weakening of snow layers may be noticeable over a period of days or weeks.**

Faceting
(common in thin snowpack)

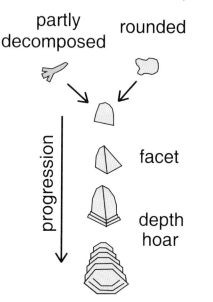

partly decomposed   rounded

progression

facet

depth hoar

Some of these large depth hoar crystals have striations (parallel growth lines.) ASARC photo.

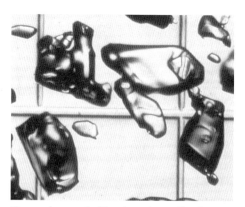

Faceted crystals like these have flat faces, edges and corners. Chris Stethem photo.

Temperature gradient

The temperature gradient determines whether a layer will be strengthened by rounding or weakened by faceting. The temperature gradient is the vertical change in temperature within the snowpack. For example, if a 10 cm (4") thick layer is -3°C (27°F) on the bottom and -5°C (23°F) on top, then the temperature gradient within that layer is 2°C per 10 cm (4°F per 4").

Consider a snow layer, which like most layers in mid-winter, is somewhat cooler on top than on the bottom. If the temperature difference between the top and bottom of the layer is large, the gradient will draw water vapor up through the snow layer, causing faceting of the grains and probably weakening of the layer. If, however, there is little temperature difference between the top and bottom of the layer, the temperature gradient will not draw water vapor through the snow fast enough to cause faceting; the grains will become rounder and the layer will strengthen.

Melt-Freeze Metamorphism

When snow is warmed to 0°C (32°F) by rain, solar radiation or warm air, rounded grains develop which are joined into clusters by liquid water. This grain structure is weak, but it forms a comparatively strong crust when the layer is refrozen. In the spring, when melt-freeze cycles are repeated daily, the resulting *spring snow* has a coarse-grained appearance.

Melt-freeze
(common during thaws, spring)

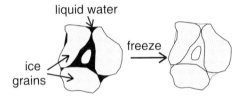

Liquid water between the grains has frozen, forming strong bonds in this melt-freeze particle. ASARC photo.

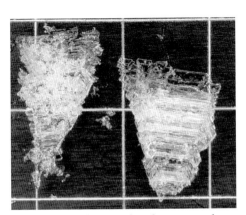

These 15 mm long surface hoar crystals formed on the snow surface. Partly because of their size, they will be slow to change by rounding or faceting. ASARC photo.

Appendix C
Avalanche Danger Scales

Canadian Avalanche Danger Scale (1996)
Avalanche safety basics

Avalanches don't happen by accident and most human involvement is a matter of **choice**, not chance. Most avalanche accidents are caused by **slab** avalanches which are triggered by the victim or by a member of the victim's party. However, **any** avalanche may cause injury or death and even small slides may be dangerous. Hence, always practise safe route-finding skills, be aware of changing conditions, and carry avalanche rescue gear. Learn and apply avalanche terrain analysis and snow stability evaluation techniques to help minimize your risk. Remember that avalanche danger rating levels are only general guidelines. Distinctions between geographic areas, elevations, slope aspects and slope angles are approximate and transition zones between dangers exist.

Canadian Avalanche Danger Descriptors (1996)

Danger Level (& Color)	Avalanche Probability and Avalanche Trigger	Recommended Action in the Backcountry
…WHAT…	…WHY…	…WHAT TO DO…
LOW (green)	Natural avalanches very unlikely. Human-triggered avalanches **unlikely**.	Travel is generally safe. Normal caution advised.
MODERATE (yellow)	Natural avalanches unlikely. Human-triggered avalanches **possible**.	Use caution in steeper terrain on certain aspects (defined in accompanying statement).
CONSIDERABLE (orange)	Natural avalanches possible. Human-triggered avalanches **probable**.	Be increasingly cautious in steeper terrain.
HIGH (red)	Natural and human-triggered avalanches **likely**.	Travel in avalanche terrain is not recommended.
EXTREME (red with black border)	Widespread natural or human-triggered avalanches **certain**.	Travel in avalanche terrain should be avoided and travel confined to low angle terrain well away from avalanche runouts.

United States Avalanche Danger Scale (1998)
Avalanche safety basics

Avalanches don't happen by accident, and most human involvement is a matter of choice, not chance. Most avalanche accidents are caused by slab avalanches which are triggered by the victim or a member of the victim's party. However, any avalanche may cause injury or death and even small slides may be dangerous. Hence, always practice safe route finding skills, be aware of changing conditions, and carry avalanche rescue gear. Learn and apply avalanche terrain analysis and snow stability evaluation techniques to help minimize your risk. Remember that avalanche danger rating levels are only general guidelines. Distinctions between geographic areas, elevations, slope aspects and slope angles are approximate and transition zones between dangers exist. No matter what the current avalanche danger there are avalanche-safe areas in the mountains.

United States Avalanche Danger Descriptors

Danger Level (& Color)	Avalanche Probability and Avalanche Trigger	Degree and Distribution of Avalanche Danger	Recommended Action in the Backcountry
…WHAT…	…WHY…	…WHERE…	…WHAT TO DO…
LOW (green)	Natural avalanches very unlikely. Human-triggered avalanches **unlikely**.	Generally stable snow. Isolated areas of instability.	Travel is generally safe. Normal caution advised.
MODERATE (yellow)	Natural avalanches unlikely. Human-triggered avalanches **possible**.	Unstable slabs **possible** on steep terrain.	Use caution in steeper terrain on certain aspects (defined in accompanying statement).
CONSID-ERABLE (orange)	Natural avalanches possible. Human-triggered avalanches **probable**.	Unstable slabs **probable** on steep terrain.	Be increasingly cautious in steeper terrain.
HIGH (red)	Natural and human-triggered avalanches **likely**.	Unstable slabs **likely** on a variety of aspects and slope angles.	Travel in avalanche terrain is not recommended. Safest travel on windward ridges of lower angle slopes without steeper terrain above.
EXTREME (block)	Widespread natural or human-triggered avalanches **certain**.	Extremely unstable slabs certain on most aspects and slope angles. Large destructive avalanches possible.	Travel in avalanche terrain should be avoided and travel confined to low-angle terrain well away from avalanche runouts.

Appendix D
Classifying the Size of Avalanches

Canadian Classification for Avalanche Size[6]

Size	Destructive Potential
1	Relatively harmless to people.
2	Could bury, injure or kill a person.
3	Could bury and destroy a car, damage a truck, destroy a small building, or break a few trees.
4	Could destroy a railway car, large truck, several buildings, or a forest area up to 4 hectares (~10 acres).
5	Largest snow avalanche known. Could destroy a village or a forest of 40 hectares (~100 acres).

Half-sizes from 1.5 to 4.5 may be used for avalanches that are between two size classes.

United States Classification for Avalanche Size[6]

Size	Description
1	Sluff or snow that slides less than 50 m (150') of slope distance, regardless of snow volume.
2	Small, relative to path.
3	Medium, relative to path.
4	Large, relative to path.
5	Major or maximum, relative to path.

Appendix E
Equipment Checklist
for Day Trip

Personal gear

beacon, probe, shovel
backpack or balloon pack
proper clothing, helmet
spare clothing
food and water
sunscreen
toilet paper
medications/prescription eyewear
headlamp, spare batteries, bulb
goggles &/or sunglasses
pocket knife/multi-tool

Group & survival gear

extra key
first aid kit
knife, saw
light rope
map, compass, altimeter
GPS receiver & spare batteries
waterproof matches, fire starter
high-energy food/bars
extra water or small pot
flashlight, flares/strobe
emergency shelter, space blankets
signal mirror
cell/satellite phone & spare batteries
emergency phone numbers for the area
spare beacon
florescent tape/flagging

First aid supplies

triangular bandages
pressure bandage
gauze pads (small & large)
adhesive bandages (small & large)
roll gauze (small & large)
alcohol wipes
antiseptic wipes
antibiotic ointment
butterfly bandages
aspirin or acetaminophen tablets
mouth-to-mouth barrier
latex gloves
micropore tape
razor/knife
scissors
needle and thread
tweezers
versatile splinting material

Sled gear

screwdrivers
pliers, wrenches (standard, allen, etc.)
spark plug wrench
spare spark plugs and drive belt
emergency starter rope
electrical tape, duct tape
wire
tow rope
gas, gas line antifreeze
misc. nuts & bolts, cotter pins
small parts common to your sled

Appendix F
Incident Response

This form can be carried in your first aid kit and used at a backcountry incident. Remember to calmly assess the situation, appoint a leader and—if safety permits—locate victims and provide first aid. If additional help is required, decide who should stay at the accident site and who should seek assistance, and send this completed form out with the messengers.

Date: Time: Terrain:	
Accident location (mark on map):	
Possible location for helicopter to land (GPS coords. or mark on map):	
Phone numbers or radio frequencies:	
Description of accident:	
Number of **injured persons**: First injured person	Second injured person
Name: age:	
Condition:	
Length of time unconscious:	
Medical history (e.g. diabetes)	
Injury 1: Treatment & needs:	
Injury 2: Treatment & needs:	
Number of **uninjured persons**: General condition: Requirements: water food shelter warm clothing Transportation options, e.g. sleds disabled	

The Authors

Bruce Jamieson recalls the thrill of riding a 6 hp snowmobile in 1963. His passion for the outdoors drew him to the mountains and snow slopes. He has been involved in avalanche safety training since 1975. Bruce worked in avalanche forecasting and control for six years, and was president of the Canadian Avalanche Association for three years. Since 1998, he has led the ASARC avalanche research group at the University of Calgary. Currently, he rides a sled—with more than 6 hp—to snow study sites in the Columbia Mountains.

Lori Zacaruk is a graduate of the Canadian Avalanche Association's first Level 2 Industry Training Program for Snowmobile Operators. She was a board member of the Canadian Avalanche Association and Canadian Avalanche Centre from 2003 to 2006.

Lori and Randy Zacaruk of Zac's Tracs are an internationally recognized avalanche safety training team bringing lifesaving skills to the snowmobile community. Zac's Tracs has received awards from the Canadian Avalanche Association (CAA), the Alberta Snowmobile Association (ASA) and most recently the Canadian Council of Snowmobile Organizations for their commitment.

Their hands-on training programs and seminars as well as the collaborative efforts with the CAA and the ASA have improved the effectiveness of national training materials, decision making tools and educational programs.

Darcy Svederus has been snow-mobiling since his early teens and is an avid mountain rider. He has been involved with the Alberta Snowmobile Association and Canadian Avalanche Association for several years and supports their programs. He started teaching Snowmobile Safety in 1994 and Avalanche Awareness in 1996. The fun still continues today.

E-mail snowtec@telus.net

About the front cover

Cover photo by Dusty Viedeman of the Revelstoke Snowmobile Club, a group which believes that everyone sledding in high country should be equipped with a transceiver, shovel and probe. Dusty had just evaluated the snow conditions and decided the slope was unsafe. He started to tell his partner—who was keen on attempting the slope—when other riders triggered it. The photo was taken a couple of minutes later when the riders started to dig out their sleds.